H O O K E D

JOE S. MCILHANEY, JR., MD AND FREDA MCKISSIC BUSH, MD

H O O K E D

NEW SCIENCE ON HOW CASUAL SEX IS AFFECTING OUR CHILDREN

NORTHFIELD PUBLISHING

CHICAGO

Editor: Pamela J. Pugh
Interior Design: Ragont Design
Cover Design: The DesignWorksGroup, Inc.

Library of Congress Cataloging-in-Publication Data

McIlhaney, Joe S.
        Hooked: New science on how casual sex is affecting our children / by Joe S. McIlhaney and Freda McKissic Bush.
            p. cm.
        Includes bibliographical references.
        ISBN-13: 978-0-8024-5060-9
        ISBN-10: 0-8024-5060-1
        1. Teenagers—Sexual behavior. 2. Children—Sexual behavior. 3. Adolescent psychology. 4. Child psychology. 5. Interpersonal relations in adolescence. 6. Interpersonal relations in children. I. Bush, Freda McKissic. II. Title.

    HQ27.M39 2008
    306.70835—dc22
                        2008009821

We hope you enjoy this book from Northfield Publishing. Our goal is to provide high-quality, thought-provoking books and products that connect truth to your real needs and challenges. For more information on our other books and products, go to www.moodypublishers.com or write to:

Northfield Publishing
820 N. LaSalle Boulevard
Chicago, IL 60610

5 7 9 10 8 6 4

Printed in the United States of America

CONTENTS

Introducing Hooked   7

1. Let's Talk Sex   11

2. Meet the Brain   25

3. The Developing Brain and Sex   49

4. Baggage Claim   73

5. Thinking Long-term   93

6. The Pursuit of Happiness   111

7. Final Thoughts   133

Acknowledgments   141

Notes   145

Index   167

INTRODUCING
HOOKED

One of the most intriguing aspects of the world around us and of our own lives is the subject of sexuality. How do we decide to engage in sex, and how do we select a partner? What does sex do to a relationship? What about sexually transmitted diseases, or teen pregnancy? How can we understand our own sexual urges, our own hopes for committed relationships and intact families, when we live in a society that sensationalizes sex and encourages us to experiment with it before we have matured enough to find our own identity?

Sixteen years ago, Joe McIlhaney, M.D., founded The Medical Institute for Sexual Health to study the science of human sexual behavior and its consequences. For much of its history, the organization has concentrated on the two primary factors that can impair sexual health: nonmarital pregnancy and sexually transmitted infections. But today, with this book, Dr. McIlhaney and his coauthor Freda McKissic Bush, M.D., reveal a third risk, one that cannot be prevented with condoms, contraceptives, or morning-after pills.

Modern neuroscience research has uncovered startling new information about how sex affects our brains. The effect of sex on our brains can have all sorts of consequences, including many that scientists are still working to understand. But we do know that sex can literally change a person's brain, influencing the thought process and affecting future decisions. And therein lies both the benefit and the risk. When sex is experienced in healthy ways it adds great value and satisfaction to life, but when experienced in unhealthy ways, at the wrong time, it can damage vital aspects of who we are as human beings.

The logical solution to these problems with sexual health is to expand our understanding of human behavior. Some of our behavior undermines even our best intentions to be healthy. Thus, this book takes a look at the unfolding scientific evidence that can help us understand sexual behavior. Once we are armed with information, then there is a fighting chance that we can work individually and as a society to bring about a new kind of sexual revolution, one that truly values sexual health.

Is this possible? We earnestly believe so. Consider the changes we have seen just in my lifetime. When I entered medical school more than forty years ago, people could smoke cigarettes on airplanes, in hospitals, even in doctors' offices. In fact, your doctor may have been smoking as he discussed your diagnosis with you. Today, that is unthinkable!

It is amazing that this cultural change has occurred despite the overwhelming influence of the tobacco industry, the acceptance of smoking by society, and the addiction of millions of men and women to the nicotine in cigarettes. Yet people learned that their behavior was indeed harmful and chose in increasing numbers to avoid the consequences: lung cancer, emphysema, heart disease, stroke, and more.

We earnestly believe change is possible for the group at greatest risk and highest potential: our young people. The following chapters discuss the development of the adolescent brain and how it is uniquely moldable and receptive to ideas and behaviors. This is especially true with regard to sex, an action that an adolescent body may desire but for which the adolescent mind may not be prepared. This book is designed to speak to parents, teachers, mentors, and young people themselves in plain language and without pretense.

At The Medical Institute for Sexual Health, we endeavor to find truth on issues of sexual health. We want everyone to be fully informed with the most credible scientific information available on issues of sexual behavior and sexual health. We want everyone to be aware of the options that offer the very best chance to have a healthy, successful life; to reach their full potential, free from the repercussions that often accompany poor sexual health decisions.

It is our hope that this book will shed new light on perplexing problems and behaviors. With new insight, perhaps we can not only better understand ourselves and our behavior, but positively impact the emotional and sexual health of the current and future generations.

Gary L. Rose, M.D.
President/CEO
The Medical Institute for Sexual Health
Austin, Texas

POPULAR CULTURE WOULD HAVE US
believe that young people should become
involved in sex when they feel ready, and
that with proper precautions, everything
will be fine.

But the facts tell a very different story.

Chapter One

LET'S TALK SEX

> "Why not? I wore a condom. She said she wanted to. We're old enough and smart enough to make decisions for ourselves. I'm not a kid anymore."
>
> —Ryan, 16

Sex!

It's everywhere. We human beings are made so that even the topic of sex gets our attention. Why? Because, as new research indicates, our interest in sex is built into our brains.

And this fascination with sex is absolutely vital. If we did not have this inborn interest in things sexual we would not have the audacity to overcome our natural hesitation to become very personal with someone else, completely intimate, and literally joined with another.

Because of our pervasive interest, society uses sex in many ways. It is one of the constant themes to which persons of all ages are exposed. Sex is used to sell music and clothes to teens, and to sell movies, automobiles, health and fitness equipment, and many other items to adults. This phenomenon has only increased over the years, aided by the Internet as well as ever-declining standards in entertainment and public discourse.

Teenagers and young adults are told that there are risks to having sex—namely, they could contract a sexually transmitted disease or they could get pregnant. These risks are well known and widely documented. However, teens and adults also know that with the use of condoms or other contraceptive techniques, the morning-after pill, vaccines, careful partner selection, and—truthfully—pure luck, it is possible to avoid these problems. Even though these physical risks are real, are dangerous, and will not be eliminated in the foreseeable future, some people are willing to accept or ignore the dangers and plunge into the lifestyle of one partner this year (or today) and another next year (or tomorrow).

> *Scientists are now beginning to see and understand results of sexual involvement that can last a lifetime.*

But is that all there is to it? Can we really warn young people about the two risks mentioned above—STDs and pregnancy—and count on current and future technology to improve their chances of avoiding them? Or are there other risks lying in wait out there—risks of problems that may not be as physically obvious but nevertheless just as devastating to an individual's freedom of opportunity in the future?

The answer is yes. Scientists are only just now beginning to be able to see and understand what we'll refer to as the third risk.

In the following chapters, we will explore

- various aspects of sexual involvement with another person;
- the results of that behavior on the brain that can

last for a lifetime after intimate contact;

- the addictive nature of sex for those involved in a series of short-term hookups or patterns of concurrent relationships leading to unhealthy choices;
- the addictive nature of sex in the context of maintaining a loving marriage;
- the fact that human beings are not slaves to the natural and good physical and emotional desire for sex;
- the fact that our brains allow us to exercise sound judgment; and
- how this capacity for good decision making can trump impulse if we practice the habit of letting it do so.

> "He was my first serious boyfriend and I thought I loved him. I really thought if I didn't have sex with him he would leave me. I was fifteen and I'd never had those kinds of feelings for anyone. I can never get that first time back."
>
> — Carrie, 19

Awakening

For prepubescent boys and girls, sexual things are asleep. The phrase "sexual awakening" is often used to describe the time in a young person's life when he or she discovers sexual interests. The term "awakening" implies that something was asleep and indeed, for younger children, this is an accurate observation. Little boys' and little girls' bodies look much the same, and they reflect the sexual immaturity of their minds. They may be curious about their own bodies, and the bodies of their parents, or have questions about where babies come from, but they lack the interest and physical development that defines a human being who is equipped for sex and childbearing.

Puberty is the time of life when boys and girls begin to physically change and develop into adults with sexual desires. The physical changes that define puberty are driven by the sex hormones: estrogen for girls and testosterone for boys. These hormones begin to be produced in increasing quantities, on average, between ages nine and eleven for girls, and ten and thirteen for boys.[1] These hormones, which are released by the ovaries or testes into the bloodstream, trigger all kinds of fascinating changes. Girls develop breasts, their hips grow wider, and they begin the menstrual cycle. Boys grow taller, their shoulders broaden, and they start growing more hair in various places on their bodies. And puberty, the doorway to adolescence, is the time when male and female reproductive organs develop to maturity.

But puberty signals far more than a physical change. There are mental and emotional transitions that accompany all of the growth and development of the body. Though the changes that puberty produces in the brain cannot be seen by anyone but neuroscientists, no one who has been around a young person going through this transition doubts that profound mental, emotional, and psychological changes are taking place at this time. Included in this change is the sudden emergence of sexual awareness, which can be an emotional roller coaster for any adolescent.

> "I couldn't wait to have sex with her. All my friends were doing it. I was tired of listening to everyone else's stories. I wanted to know what it was like for myself."
>
> —Kevin, 17

Healthy Appetites

Sex can be considered one of the appetites with which we are born. If you look up "appetite" in Merriam-Webster's Dictionary, you'll read that it's "any of the instinctive desires necessary to keep up organic life." A secondary definition is "an inherent craving." A truth to remember is that appetites are *necessary* but are values-neutral. They can be used appropriately or they can be misunderstood and misused. For example, without an appetite for food, we wouldn't survive. Food provides energy and fuels our bodies. Yet misuse of this natural appetite in the forms of overeating or eating too much of the wrong things, for example, can cause problems such as cardiovascular disease, diabetes, and many others.

These health problems can dramatically change the entire course of an individual's life.

Sex is an important, healthy appetite that fits perfectly the definition of "an instinctive desire necessary to keep up organic life." Without an appetite for sex, there would be no procreation, and human life would come to an end. But as with food, sex can be misunderstood and misused. We can see the physical damage to health from the misuse of sex— HIV/AIDS and sexually transmitted diseases. These are not insignificant problems—they occur far more often than most people realize.[2]

And when they do occur, they can change the entire course of a person's life.

In contrast to pregnancy or sexually transmitted disease, the emotional and psychological impact of sex cannot be guarded against with condoms or other forms of contraception. This is a third risk of sex, one that is rarely acknowledged but that has enormous implications for young people and their futures. You'll read about it in this book.

So, when is it "sex"?

So now that we know that sex is a normal appetite, what exactly is it? As strange as it sounds, many people disagree over what sex really is. For example, does penetration have to occur in order for the act to qualify as "sex"? Or can two people "have sex" simply by touching each other, even on top of their clothes? Does oral sex count? What about masturbation? The most reasonable definition suggested by recent brain studies indicates that *sexual activity is any intimate contact between two individuals that involves arousal, stimulation, and/or a response by at least one of the two partners.*

> "Sex is when you go all the way with somebody. As long as you don't actually do it, you aren't having sex. So we can still have a good time without worrying about all that other stuff."
>
> —Melissa, 15

In other words, sexual activity is any intentionally sexual intimate behavior between two partners, or even one person if self-stimulation is used.

However, sexual arousal does not *begin* with the parts of your body that feel the most aroused. Sexual excitement is actually centered in the brain. It is possible to be stimulated and even achieve orgasm without any physical contact with the sexual organs at all. An excellent example of this is a nocturnal emission known as a "wet dream"—when arousal and even ejaculation occurs in dreams during sleep.

> *Modern brain scan technology shows different areas of the brain lighting up.*

Perhaps the best way to describe how sex begins in the brain is to consider a couple and go through the typical sequence of events that leads them to sexual intercourse, assuming the relationship is nonabusive and unselfish. There is usually a progression of physical contact that, sooner or later, acquires the *purpose* of having sexual intercourse. A couple may begin with touching, light kissing, and other behaviors not commonly referred to as sex. This fascinating process is clearly visible with modern brain scan technology, revealing different areas of the brain "lighting up." The couple who has already established sex as part of their relationship may not have begun touching with the intention of having sex, but at some point that can become the goal. At that time, the kissing, touching, and any other contact takes on a new energy, and different portions of the brain become engaged and aroused. When those actions are taken with the *intention* of having sex, sexual activity has begun, concluding with physical sexual union.

We can also see from this description why it is necessary to include conduct such as showering together, oral sex, mutual masturbation, and heavy petting as sexual activity.[3] In addition to being included as sexual behavior because of the intent of either or both people involved, these are sexual behaviors because, among other things, they can result in a person becoming infected with a sexually transmitted infection if he or she engages in some of these activities with an infected person.[4] These behaviors are also considered sexual activity since the individuals involved can experience similar emotions of excitement and pleasure as they would from other sexual activity, as well as experience devastation when the relationship with the person with whom they've engaged in these activities ends.

Integrating all this information leads us to the conclusion that a definition of sexual activity must include not only sexual intercourse, but also anal sex, oral sex, mutual masturbation, showering together, fondling of breasts, other behaviors and, yes, even kissing if done purposely to produce sexual stimulation and gratification.

Sex can and should be a positive experience. It should be the intimate interaction between two persons who care for each other and desire to share their innermost feelings with each other. Sex has many wonderful benefits: the pleasure and satisfaction of becoming an intimate part of another person's body; verbal and physical communication; expressing and deriving pleasure with a partner; uniting the "two" to become another "one" and, clearly, the potential for procreation

But sex misused has obvious negative consequences. When one is forced or coerced to have sex, it is not good. When sex is used to accomplish favors or to influence another, it is not good. When sex is used for financial gain, used abusively, or used to humiliate another, it is not good. When sex results in an unplanned, nonmarital pregnancy or a sexually transmitted infection, it is not good. And when sex produces feelings of regret, depression, suicidal ideation and other emotional problems, it is not good.

> "I had no idea how having sex as a teenager could affect the rest of my life. I didn't really know what love was. By the time I got married, sex was so confusing for me. It has been a huge issue in our marriage and I don't know how to fix it."
>
> —Christie, 29

Not just a body

Now that we have defined sex according to physical activity—according to what our bodies are doing—we're ready to talk about the rest of the story. In order to truly understand why sex sells and why it is so pervasive in our society, we have to understand that humans are not just sex machines or animals. We, as human beings, are so much more.

If we think of sex as only a physical activity to be engaged in at our pleasure, and only for our pleasure, we will be blindsided by problems produced by the misunderstandings and miscalculations of our human nature. If we think our makeup is limited to satisfying appetites, we'll conclude that we can engage in sexual activity, enjoy it on a physical level, and totally disassociate these acts from the rest of what we are as human beings—but we'll be sadly mistaken.

Going back to the time of sexual awakening, important research into the phenomenon of puberty has yielded some important discoveries. It has been found that in situations with poor or unhealthy parent-teenager relations, teenage boys with high testosterone levels were more likely to engage in risky behavior of all kinds, including sex.[5] Teenage girls with poor parental relationships were more likely to engage in similar risky behavior. Yet in each case, research has found that home environment had greater influence on behavior than hormone levels and if parent-child relations were good, hormone levels do not seem to matter at all regarding risky sexual behavior.[6]

So what's the point? It is worth remembering that every child's body and brain transforms as he or she gets older, and this transformation has a huge physical and psychological impact on all things sexual. An intense fascination and desire for sex often accompanies these changes. Yet simply going through puberty, or having a sex hormone coursing through a young person's bloodstream, does not determine the decisions they make about sex. Beneficial factors, such as home environment and adult guidance, can shepherd an adolescent through this tumultuous period in life. Negative guidance, if it dominates, from peers or the media can make the journey much more difficult.[7]

Finally, it is clear that the brain is still developing during puberty, and will continue to do so far after the external physical changes have reached their conclusion.

One recent study of sexually active adolescents illustrates that sexual activity has more ramifications beyond the physical. The study showed that both boys and girls who have had sex are three times more likely to be depressed than their friends who are still virgins. The study accounted for other factors in the lives of the young people, ensuring an accurate comparison with their peers. The girls who became sexually active were three times more likely to have attempted suicide as their virgin friends, while the sexually active boys were fully seven times more likely to have attempted suicide.[8]

Yet it is a good bet that none of these young people were aware that depression and suicidal thoughts might be caused in part by their sexual behavior. Consider the following questions:

- Why are those who were not virgins when they married more likely to divorce than those who remained abstinent until marriage? [9]
- Why are sexually active adolescents more likely to be depressed than their abstaining peers? [10]
- Why do married couples report higher levels of sexual satisfaction than unmarried individuals with multiple sexual partners?[11]

The answers, of course, lie in the fact that human beings are creatures who are much more than physical bodies. We possess the ability for cognitive thought, which includes judgment, abstract thinking, planning for the future, moral intelligence, and other processes that govern our lives. Our decision-making ability, coming from the highest centers of the brain, can guide an individual to the most rewarding sexual behavior—unless bad programming from premature and unwise sexual behavior during the adolescent years has occurred, causing the brain formation for healthy decision making to be damaged.[12]

This is a risk about which most young people and most parents are totally unaware.

Fortunately, modern neuroscience of the past few years has opened a door of understanding that provides incredibly helpful guidance away from trouble. Many of the answers to the questions above, and others, may be found in modern neuroscientific research, the study of the human brain and nervous system, which has revealed startling new information about how sex affects the brain.

Until now, efforts to accurately assess the connection between sex, love, sexual desire, sexual risk-taking, and so on with brain activity have been limited. But with the aid of modern research techniques and technologies, scientists are confirming that sex is more than a momentary physical act. It produces powerful, even lifelong, changes in our brains that direct and influence our future to a surprising degree.[13] This new neuroscience information, which has only become widely available in the last decade, has transformed the scientific discussion about sex. Perspectives from medical, public health, and social science literature will also be utilized in this book to enhance our understanding of sexual behavior in adolescents and young adults in the larger cultural context.

The uniqueness of becoming an intimate part of another person's mind—emotional bonding and the vital role this plays in one's health, happiness, and hope for the future—

is the central issue we will be explaining in this book. It is probably the most important outcome of healthy, positive sex.

♦ How can "sexual activity" be defined? How do the authors arrive at this description?

♦ When is sex a positive experience? When is it not?

♦ How are humans more than a collection of physical body parts?

MOST OF US DON'T CONSIDER
what our complex, three-pound brain
has to do with our sex life.

Chapter Two

MEET THE BRAIN

Some individuals have been disappointed to find as they move from one sexual partner to another, that not only are they not finding ultimate pleasure but they are feeling worse about themselves and their many sexual partners. They wonder why they feel this way.[1]

At the same time, for a married couple sex is often spoken of as the deepest level of communication. It is seen and felt as a bonding experience by them and central to a healthy relationship.[2]

What is going on? How can this be? Can sex be a healthy, relationship-building experience for married couples, but only a physical encounter for single people just "hooking up"?

The Brain: A Sex Organ?

Until just a few years ago, scientists, psychologists, and physicians had little in the way of research and data to connect the dots. They knew instinctively, just as countless generations of sexually experienced people did, that sex is more than just a physical experience. They knew it engaged the mind in powerful, if largely unknown, ways. But they had no way of really knowing what was happening in the brain when people experienced love, passion, lust, sex, or other emotions and activities.

Today, however, thanks to breakthroughs in neuroscience research techniques, scientists have been able to literally view the activity of the brain as it functions. With state-of-the-art mapping and imaging tools, researchers have unlocked a new world of data on what happens between your ears each day.[3]

In addition, new methods of tracking brain chemicals have allowed scientists to understand when and how much of these chemicals are released and how they influence behavior. We now have scientific studies about brain function and sexual thoughts and behavior that are not only fascinating but are true breakthroughs in our understanding of ourselves and the intriguing part of our behavior called sex.[4] And yes, this new science does establish once and for all that more happens during sex than physical activity or the transfer of secretions (or germs). What we now know from science is what some have been saying for years—that the largest and most important sex organ is the brain. To understand this, we'll need a basic understanding of the brain.

Brain Basics: Neurons, support cells, synapses

The appearance of the outside of the brain is familiar to most people. Seen in biology classrooms and in textbooks, the familiar gray lump is easily identifiable. Many have learned about the main parts of the brain and know that different parts control different functions. But most of us don't consciously consider how this complex organ functions in our daily lives.

In many ways, this is a good thing. For example, we don't have to figure out how to walk, breathe, perspire, swallow, or any number of the things we do every day, almost automatically. We don't have to stop and think how to do these things.

However, for our understanding of how we think and of our decisions about behavior, it can be exceedingly helpful to have some understanding of the internal workings of our brains and the brains of our children.

Neurons: The *neuron* is the primary cell of the brain. It is the cell through which the electricity flows that makes the brain work. A neuron consists of a cell body containing the nucleus and the surrounding fluid called the cytoplasm, which fills the neuron cell like water in a balloon. The most explicit image of the neuron is one that includes several short projections—dendrites—from the nerve cell for receiving transmissions, and one long projection—an axon—for sending transmissions.

Support Cells: By the time a person reaches the end of her adolescent years, her brain contains more than 10 billion neurons. In addition, the brain holds another 100 billion *support cells*. These cells hold the neurons together, assist in the growth and development of the neurons, and remove waste material when a neuron dies. The brain is richly supplied with blood vessels, a part of the support cell system.

Synapses: In order for the brain to function, the various neurons need to be able to communicate with one another and connect into a cohesive whole. Much like the Internet for computers, the brain's network requires connections and continuity—otherwise it would simply be a collection of dead ends. The connections that bridge the gaps between neurons are called *synapses*. The neurons in question are not seamlessly physically connected by the synapse—there is always a small gap where the electricity is carried by a neurochemical, which will be discussed later in this chapter.

> *Neurons form over 100 trillion connections with each other.*

But unlike the cables or wires that connect your home computer to the Internet, synapses are not permanent, fixed objects. They are organic connections that rely on use for their very existence. In this manner, they are somewhat like your muscles or some other kinds of organic tissue— in other words, use them or lose them.

When a new activity or experience occurs, it can result in a strengthening of the connection between neurons, or even in a new connection altogether. These connections are critical for memory, behavior, emotions, desires, and any number of other outcomes that activity or experience brings. If that experience or activity occurs again, the connection is used and strengthened in the process. If that connection is not used, the synapse eventually breaks down and dies. This process refers to either a continued connection between neurons or to a loss of connection—not the life or death of the neurons themselves, although that can and does occur as well.[5]

The neurons form over 100 trillion connections with each other—more than all the Internet connections in the world![6] The human brain is, without question, the most complicated three-pound mass of matter in the known universe.

The moldable brain

A fundamental fact about the brain i birth until death, the brain is moldable a not a rigid, immutable structure, but an and flex.

The primary things that change in the brain structure, that mold it, are its synapses. Synapses either are sustained or they are allowed to deteriorate based on behavior and experience. It may seem incredible, but the things we see, do, and experience actually cause part of our brains to flourish, i.e., synapses that survive and strengthen; and part of our brain to weaken, i.e., synapses that disintegrate or die.[8]

For example, the Chinese language does not include words with the sounds of the English letters *L* or *R*. Consequently, children raised in Chinese-speaking households neither hear nor use those sounds. The part of their brains responsible for language never uses the synapses that would allow them to pronounce *L* and *R*,[9] so those synapses wither and die. Those individuals therefore do not have the physical ability, because of the lack of nerve connections, to make the muscles of their throats, mouths, and lips make those sounds. But since the brain is moldable, people who did not grow up producing these sounds can develop new nerve connections and learn to do so, though it takes a great deal of effort and practice.

Another example that graphically illustrates the way our experience and behavior mold our brains is shown by brain imaging of violinists. Such pictures of professional violinists show that the portion of the brain that controls the fingers on their left hand (the hand that fingers the violin strings) are much larger than the same area of the brains of individuals who are not violinists.[10]

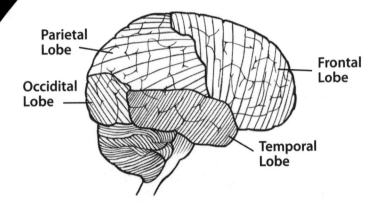

The brain and its lobes within the cerebral cortex.

In these examples, it is clear that the connections—synapses—in the human brain

- are adaptable and subject to change, and
- have enormous implications for human behavior and actions.

Neurochemicals: dopamine, oxytocin, vasopressin

As we have seen, the brain would not work without neurons, support cells, or synapses. There is a fourth absolutely essential part of the brain—its neurochemicals.

A neurochemical is one that is unique to or active in the brain. There are hundreds of these chemicals bathing the brain cells, synapses, and support cells all the time. Some of these chemicals are necessary for messages to go from one cell, across the synapse, to another cell. Without these chemicals, most messages could not move through the brain at all.

In addition to the neurochemicals necessary for moving messages along there are other neurochemicals that play amazing, exciting, and almost unbelievable roles in our thinking, desires, and behavior.

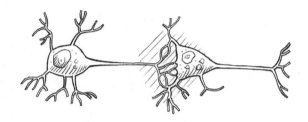

The neural circuit. This includes the neuron's cell body, the axon extending from one neuron to another, and the synapse, or connection point between two neurons in the brain. The synapse is the functional connection point between two neurons.

Some of these are very involved in our sexual interest and behavior. We will discuss the ones of most importance to our subject. Other neurohormones are also involved in sex, some produced in the brain and some from other parts of the body. Some of these are endorphins, estrogen, progesterone, testosterone, and serotonin. Discussion of all these will not significantly add to or subtract from our discussion so will not be included in this book to any extent.

Dopamine: The messenger chemical *dopamine* makes a person feel good when he or she does something exciting or rewarding. Dopamine, therefore, has great influence over human behavior. The official term for what dopamine does is "reward signal"—that is, when we do something exciting, dopamine rewards us by flooding our brains and making the brain cells produce a feeling of excitement or of well-being.

Dopamine makes us feel good because of the intense energy, exhilaration, and focused attention it produces when we do something important or stimulating. It makes us feel the need or desire to repeat pleasurable, exciting, and rewarding acts.[11]

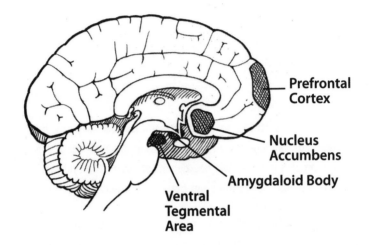

Prefrontal Cortex

Nucleus Accumbens

Amygdaloid Body

Ventral Tegmental Area

Areas of the brain that are involved with the production and transmission of dopamine. Dopamine is involved in "rewarding" the brain for risky or exhilarating behavior. This might include positive things such as good grades or negative things such as driving too fast.

We can see, therefore, that dopamine is vital to living a healthy, normal life. It is dopamine that gives us a charge of excitement and rewards us for having the courage to take an action with an uncertain outcome. It can, for example, reward someone for taking the risk of choosing to get married, have a child, start a new job or business, or other significant venture. We humans are not—and shouldn't be—averse to taking risks.

Dopamine is one of the most important messenger chemicals in the brain. It has many functions, including important roles in behavior, cognition, motor activity, and motivation and reward. Through its unique impact on the brain, dopamine helps guide human behavior. It should be noted, however, that dopamine is values-neutral. In other words, it is an involuntary response that cannot tell right from wrong, or beneficial from harmful—it rewards all kinds of behavior without distinction.

Dopamine plays a particularly powerful role in the lives and brains of adolescents. Dopamine levels reach their peak in late childhood, presumably to prepare the child's brain for the dopamine it will need during adolescence. But dopamine levels do continue to increase in one important part of the brain, the prefrontal cortex. This is the final portion of the brain to complete its development, and it is the part of the brain responsible for the mature decision making required of adults.[12]

We said earlier that dopamine plays a vital role in the normal, healthy, and important risk taking of life. Because adolescence is such a dynamic time of life change, this messenger chemical plays an especially important role for young people during this time. Consider, for example, a vital and natural, yet highly risky move for an adolescent—separating from parents to become a self-sustaining adult. Dopamine rewards the young adult for this risky venture by making him feel excited and good about achieving independence even if he does not know if he can, in fact, provide for himself.

This same risk/reward holds true for picking a lifelong mate: "What if I'm not marrying the right person?" or having a child: "Can we afford a child? Will we be good parents? What if our child has special challenges?" Countless fears that could stymie a person are overcome by dopamine, which brings excitement to these new ventures.[13]

As noted previously, dopamine is values-neutral. This important point must be stressed. Dopamine will reward for healthy and life-enhancing excitement, but it will also send the reward signal for exhilarating but unhealthy and destructive behavior.

Examples of excitement that dopamine rewards can include the use of nonprescriptive drugs, nonmarital sexual involvement, excessive drinking, dangerous thrill-seeking, and so on. The good "high" feeling these behaviors can produce can cause an adolescent (and also an adult) to want to seek more of that good feeling. To reproduce the good feeling they seek to repeat the behavior. Their desire for the good feeling can overwhelm their accurately calculating the risk of the behavior, or for that matter, even worrying about it, if they do consider the risk.[14]

An even more subtle danger regarding addictive drugs is that most of them can overstimulate the dopamine neurons and cause the brain to become relatively resistant to dopamine, thus causing the individual to seek more of the drug or of the behavior that produced the good feelings in the first place. This of course can be part of the reason why addiction to drugs or to certain behaviors occur.

Studies with animals have shown that almost all addictive drugs including alcohol, cocaine, heroine, amphetamines, and even marijuana and nicotine increase dopamine reward signals.[15]

The danger, of course, is that if young people have been receiving a dopamine reward of good feelings from dangerous behavior such as driving too fast, smoking, sex, and others, they can feel compelled to increase that behavior in order to achieve the same good feeling.[16]

There is more risk than might seem apparent from this statement. We'll go into more depth later, but remember that the brain is a moldable organ—take a heady experience such as driving fast. The behavior is exciting; it triggers a values-neutral dopamine reward, and strengthens the synapses that lead to making habitually unsafe driving decisions.

When this molding occurs as a result of the experience of driving fast, the individual can become immune to a more mature understanding that driving fast is unwise and dangerous. He or she can accept "driving fast" as normal and live life based on that assumption.[17] This same scenario can play out with alcohol, drugs, violence, or almost any other human activity.

However, sex is one of the strongest generators of the dopamine reward.[18] For this reason, young people particularly are vulnerable to falling into a cycle of dopamine reward for unwise sexual behavior—they can get hooked on it.

But the beneficial effect of dopamine for the married couple is that it "addicts" them to sex with each other.

Oxytocin: Another neurochemical that is critically important to healthy sex and bonding is *oxytocin*. While it is present in both genders, it is primarily active in females. According to the research we have today, the female body uses oxytocin at four different times. [19]

These actions of oxytocin seem at first to be arbitrary and disconnected. But look again. They all have to do with reproduction, and the nourishment of and a provision for a supportive and protective environment for a child.

REASON FOR OXYTOCIN RELEASE:	ACTION OF OXYTOCIN:
Meaningful or intimate touching with another individual	Bonding and trust in the other person
Sexual intercourse	Bonding and trust in the other person
Onset of labor in a pregnant woman	Oxytocin causes uterine contractions in association with other mechanisms, results in birth
Nipple stimulation after delivery of an infant	Helps produce the flow of milk from a mother's breast during nursing

One of the requirements for the continuation of the human race is that men and women desire to have sexual intercourse with each other. The act of intercourse results not only in a bonding of the two people, but often produces children. When the parents are truly committed and bonded together, the odds are much better that the baby will be born into a home with two parents who stay together to raise her. It is clear that oxytocin is intimately involved in all these steps. We could almost call oxytocin the neuro-hormone of life itself.

One dramatic example of the strong bonding effect of oxytocin on the mother-infant relationship occurs during breast-feeding. As a mother holds her baby skin-to-skin and nurses, her brain is being flooded with oxytocin. The presence of oxytocin produces a chemical impact on the mother's brain that makes her want to be with her baby and willing to inconvenience herself for her baby. Oxytocin is intimately involved in the bonding process between a mother and child. In the extreme circumstance of a mother giving her life for her baby, she is willing to do so not because the child is "cute," but because she is bound to that baby. The bonding effect of oxytocin is powerful. [20]

This oxytocin impact is obviously vital for the survival of human infants since they are totally unable to provide for themselves in the early years of their lives. However, without oxytocin, babies might not be conceived at all. Here is where the new research about oxytocin becomes even more interesting. When two people touch each other in a warm, meaningful, and intimate way, oxytocin is released into the woman's brain. The oxytocin then does two things: increases a woman's desire for more touch and causes bonding of the woman to the man she has been spending time in physical contact with.

This desire for more touch and the bonding that develops between a man and a woman often lead to the most intimate of physical contact, sexual intercourse. With sexual intercourse and orgasm, the woman's brain is flooded with oxytocin, causing her to desire this same kind of contact again and again with this man she has bonded to, producing even stronger bonding.[21]

But there is more. The oxytocin bonding that takes place in the normal male-female relationship often results in long-term connectedness. For example, in America, when a marriage is intact, it is rare for a woman to have sexual intercourse with anyone except her husband.[22] This remarkable stability is undoubtedly in part a result of the effect of oxytocin. And the significance of this is that the bonding of a mother and father (part of the reason marriages often last for many years) greatly increases the chance for a child to be raised in a nurturing two-parent home, which studies have shown provides a child the most advantageous environment for growing into his or her potential.[23]

The important thing to recognize is that the desire to connect is not *just* an emotional feeling. Bonding is real and almost like the adhesive effect of glue—a powerful connection that cannot be undone without great emotional pain.[24]

Real brain chemicals act on real brain cells, causing those brain cells to bind individuals together. While no one can prove exactly why the brain was made to respond to oxytocin in this way, some valid observations as to why it is important are easy to make. Simply put, the continuation of the human race has always depended on men and women forming relationships, conceiving and bearing children, and raising those children together until they can care for themselves . . . and continue the cycle.

While many scientists and behavioral experts have connected the dots and concluded that oxytocin is key to bonding a mother and child, few have appropriately emphasized the similar effect between a mother and father. Just as nature has provided a built-in defense mechanism to ensure that infants are not abandoned, it has also provided a mechanism that works to keep sexually active couples together as well.

Oxytocin, however, is values-neutral. Much like dopamine, it is an involuntary process that cannot distinguish between a one-night stand and a lifelong soul mate. Oxytocin can cause a woman to bond to a man even during what was expected to be a short-term sexual relationship. She may know he is not the man she would want to marry but intimate sexual involvement causes her to be so attached to him she can't make herself separate. This can lead to a woman being taken off-guard by a desire to stay with a man she would otherwise find undesirable and staying with him even if he is possessive or abusive.

Finally, an important finding of scientists about oxytocin is that it produces a feeling of trust in a person with whom a female is in close contact. When a woman considers engaging in sex with a man, she needs to be able to trust him. A woman who is being approached sexually by a man is very vulnerable. He is almost always stronger than she is. He could do things to her physically that she does not want. He can infect her with an STD. He also can cause her to become pregnant. If she does become pregnant and has a baby she has to trust the man to stay with her and not leave. Then she needs to trust that he will help provide food, clothing, and shelter for her and the child. Finally, she needs to trust that he will provide love and connectedness for her and the child.

On being approached by a man for sex or for marriage she may not think this far into the future or consider adverse consequences to her actions, but her trust in the man is fundamental to her joining her body to his or even joining her future to his in marriage. Oxytocin helps build this trust that is so essential to a healthy relationship.

There is a warning here for parents and young people, particularly young women. If a young woman becomes physically close to and hugs a man, it will trigger the bonding process, creating a greater desire to be near him and, most significantly, place greater trust in him. Then, if he wants to escalate the physical nature of the relationship, it will become harder and harder for her to say no.[25] The adolescent girl who enters into a close physical relationship may therefore find herself, because of the normal effect of her brain hormones, desiring more physical contact and trusting a male who may be using manipulative pledges of love and care only to get her to have sex.

Louann Brizendine, M.D., a neuropsychiatrist at the University of California, offers compelling evidence of how quickly this process can be initiated: "From an experiment on hugging, we also know that oxytocin is naturally released in the brain after a twenty-second hug from a partner—sealing the bond between the huggers and triggering the brain's trust circuits. So don't let a guy hug you unless you plan to trust him. Touching, gazing, positive emotional interaction, kissing, and sexual orgasm also release oxytocin in the female brain. Such contact may just help flip the switch on the brain's romantic love circuits."[26]

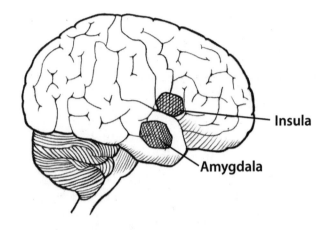

Areas within a woman's brain believed to be involved in the development of trust and trustworthiness. The brain chemical oxytocin likely plays an important role in these processes and is involved in maternal care, social attachment, and bonding. Perception of another person's face is associated with an emotional response within the amygdale. The insula helps translate this emotional response into a feeling about the person.

While the hormonal effect of oxytocin is ideal for marriage, it can cause problems for the unmarried woman or girl who is approached by a man desiring sex. Once again, the warning is that a woman's brain can cause her to be blindsided by a bad relationship that she thought was good because of the physical contact and the oxytocin response it generates. The truth about such a relationship may be apparent to parents or friends who are concerned about the girl's well-being, but it takes wisdom and tact to effectively warn a young woman about a relationship others can see could be dangerous to her.

Not all relationships, of course, are made up of a manipulative male and an unaware female, and our point is not to imply this. But young women especially need to be aware of the powerful bonding effect of oxytocin. When a couple is involved in even a short-term relationship and breaks up and then each moves on to a new sexual partner, they are breaking an oxytocin bond that has formed. This severing of the bond explains the incredibly painful emotions people often feel when they break up.[27]

In addition, they cannot know that they actually are seriously damaging a bonding mechanism that they are born with, a mechanism put there to allow them to, in the future, have a healthy bonded marriage that is a stable relationship and provides a healthy nest for children that might be conceived and born into their home, a problem we'll discuss later.

Vasopressin: Women are not the only ones who bond during intimate physical contact. The neurochemical responsible for the male brain response and synaptic change is called *vasopressin*. It plays a role in many body functions such as blood pressure regulation and, through its influence on kidney function, fluid regulation in the body. Vasopressin seems to have two primary functions related to relationships—bonding of the man to his mate and attachment to his offspring.[28]

Due to the remarkable structural similarity between oxytocin and vasopressin, it should come as no surprise that these two neurochemicals share similar activity. Often referred to as the "monogamy molecule," vasopressin seems to be the primary cause of men attaching to women with whom they have close and intimate physical contact. Vasopressin has been studied through research on prairie voles, small mammals that live in the grasslands of the Midwest and that are amazingly monogamous. These studies have shown that if the flow of vasopressin is blocked, male voles did not bond to females with whom they were sexually active.[29] However, when the male vole's brain is being flooded with adequate amounts of vasopressin, a condition that is normal for such voles, he shows increased attention and attachment to his young.[30]

Though vasopressin has not been studied as much as has oxytocin, we know it clearly plays an important role in sexual bonding and bonding between fathers and children. As with oxytocin, this mechanism is extremely important for the proper care of children. If a man and woman are emotionally bonded when pregnancy is achieved and then children are born, the children have a greater chance of being raised by their two biological parents—both of whom are attached to them—increasing their chance of survival, good health, and a productive future. Therefore, just as with oxytocin, vasopressin is vitally important to our survival as a race.

> *The inability to bond after multiple sex encounters is almost like tape that loses its stickiness after being applied and removed multiple times.*

Just like dopamine and oxytocin, vasopressin is values-neutral. If a male enters into a physical relationship with a female unwisely, he could bond to her. This bonding could lead to a long-term relationship that is unhealthy and destructive because it was an unwise relationship to start with, yet the bonding keeps the couple together, even if the man is being abused by the woman.

As with dopamine and oxytocin, vasopressin has a powerful impact on human behavior. Yet most people are totally unaware of it. Men may question why they keep going back to a woman who treats them poorly or may wonder why they never seem able to feel, deep inside, a commitment to a woman after having sex partner after sex partner. Sadly, they simply do not know that their brains are flooded with vasopressin during sexual intercourse and that this neurochemical produces a partial bond with every woman they have sex with. They do not realize that this pattern of having sex with one woman and then breaking up and then having sex with another woman limits them to experience only one form of brain activity common to humans involved sexually—the dopamine rush of sex.[31] They risk damaging a vital, innate ability to develop the long-term emotional attachment that results from sex with the same person over and over. This transition can be seen in the brain studies of individuals who have been involved with each other for a period of months.[32] The individual who goes from sex partner to sex partner is causing his or her brain to mold and gel so that it eventually begins accepting that sexual pattern as normal. For most people this brain pattern seems to interfere with the development of the neurological circuits necessary for the long-term relationships that for most people result in stable marriages and family development. The pattern of changing sex partners therefore seems to damage their ability to bond in a committed relationship.[33]

Their inability to bond after multiple liaisons is almost like tape that loses its stickiness after being applied and removed multiple times.

Scent sense: pheromones

Pheromones are chemicals secreted by the skin and sweat glands of many animals and of human males and females. When they are inhaled through the nose, they can stimulate surprising and unexpected thoughts, feelings, and behavioral responses. They are unconsciously detectable to the female nose (but not the male nose) and can have a powerful psychological and behavioral impact.[34]

Pheromones are transmitted through scent, although they do not carry an odor that humans can consciously detect. Research has revealed that pheromones are involved in a woman's sexual attraction for a specific type of man. We also know that pheromones are involved, to some unknown extent, with a woman's sexual satisfaction with a man.[35] And all of this is unconscious influence, much like the impact of dopamine, oxytocin, and other neurochemicals.

Pheromones obviously do not overwhelm all other factors that influence sexual behavior choices. They are, however, one more piece of evidence in the case we are building that powerful influences are at work regarding sexual behavior choices. Most of us think of our choices as being influenced by some kind of love or emotional feeling. Instead, it can be strongly influenced by a neurochemical, pheromonal, or other effect that requires clear-headed discernment to understand.

The brain is involved in our decisions about sex and the actions that follow, far beyond what is apparent.

That discernment is provided by the mature cognitive thought and control of the prefrontal cortex and, in the case of adolescents, buttressed by the advice and guidance of parents and other caring adults.

More than a feeling

It has often been said that a human's largest sexual organ is the brain. It is certainly the most complicated, and it is responsible for activities and effects that go far beyond the momentary pleasure of sex.

We've seen how the brain is composed of multiple neurons, all of which are connected by synapses. These synapses can be created, grow, or deteriorate based on our thoughts and actions. In this manner, each person actually changes the very structure of the brain with the choices he or she makes and the behavior he or she is involved in.

We've also seen how our choices are affected by chemicals in our brains. These chemicals are in place for important reasons, and have much to do with the survival of the human race. Dopamine floods our brains and rewards us for exciting or risky behavior—like growing up and separating from our parents, committing to another person in marriage, or birthing and raising children. Oxytocin helps females become attached to men, have children, and bond with those children, thus giving them the greatest chance for a healthy future. In like manner, vasopressin helps men become attached to a woman and to their children.

Taken as a whole, these complicated processes offer a compelling pattern. They are designed to lead toward and strengthen long-term monogamous relationships, supporting and reinforcing the family structure that is so vital to our survival.

However, we have also seen that these chemicals and processes are values-neutral. They can produce involuntary responses that result in all kinds of behavior, including activities that are dangerous or unwise.

The brain, then, is very involved in our decisions about sex and the actions that follow, far beyond what is apparent on the surface. We know that nonmarital sexual activity can produce sexually transmitted infection and unplanned pregnancy, but it is just as clear that some of the most powerful effects of sex are emotional and psychological. Next, we'll see what this means for young people whose brains and bodies are still growing and developing.

to THINK ABOUT

♦ What do the authors mean by "use them or lose them," referring to synapses? What do synapses have to do with the brain being moldable?

♦ What does it mean to call dopamine and other neuro-chemicals "values-neutral"?

♦ How are oxytocin and vasopressin bonding chemicals?

THE BRAIN CAN BE MOLDED POSITIVELY
by structure and guidance.
It can also be molded negatively by
poor input.

What is certain is that the brain will be
molded by one or the other.

Chapter Three

THE DEVELOPING BRAIN AND SEX

> **"I wish I had said no. I wish I had been strong enough, and I wish my parents had helped me more. I had no idea that having sex would change my life so much."**
>
> —Karen, 20

We've already gotten a glimpse of how the three-pound human brain is the most complex mass of matter in the universe. But just how does the brain develop? Can anything influence brain development for better or for worse? And how does the topic of sex fit into this discussion?

We're all familiar with the external signs of physical growth as a person goes from babyhood through childhood and adolescence: loose teeth, shoes that don't fit anymore, clumsiness, and a voracious appetite, just to name a few. But how does the growth process affect the brain? After all, just as the rest of the body does, the human brain itself grows and develops from birth to adulthood. The maturation of the brain is in many ways more delicate, more unpredictable, more important, and until recently, less understood than that of any other part of the body.

For many parents of adolescents, the phenomenon of the developing brain can be summarized in a single question:

"Why in the world does my teenager act this way?" Historically, the scientific community was not able to respond to that question very well. In the past, most of the techniques for studying the adolescent brain were invasive or potentially damaging. Therefore, little was known about the activity going on inside a young person's brain.[1]

> "I want to protect my kids. I would never want them to go through what I did, and have to live with the guilt and regret. I wouldn't wish it on anybody, least of all them."
>
> —Mark, 36

Inside the adolescent brain

Only during the past few years have scientists been able to use new technologies such as MRI (Magnetic Resonance Imaging), fMRI (functional MRI), and PET (positron emission tomography scans) to study the brain in groundbreaking new ways. The technology called *MRI*, which relies on magnets instead of X-rays, has revealed amazing new information about adolescent brain activity. Since magnets do not hurt living tissue and therefore can be used over and over, this technology can be used to observe adolescent brains as they grow and develop.

A *functional MRI* uses similar technology to observe how much oxygen a given portion of the brain is using. When an area of the brain is "working," it must have oxygen to fuel that work. That increased oxygen consumption is measured by functional MRI, revealing new data about what is happening in the brain.

A *PET scan* is a medical imaging technique that produces a three-dimensional image or map of the brain by measuring the flow of blood to any given area. When an area of the brain is active, there is more blood flow, and the PET scanner can "see" that. For example, one fascinating finding reports that the brain center for "lust" is different than the brain center for "love." Knowledge of this phenomenon is made possible by PET scans and other new techniques.[2]

Primarily with the aid of MRI, scientists have made an important discovery about the brain's growth and maturation. The part of the brain that controls the ability to make fully mature judgment decisions is not physically mature until an individual reaches his mid-twenties. In other words, the part of a brain that is responsible for complex assessments about future consequences and responsibility is still growing throughout the teen years and into the mid-twenties.[3]

Most of us give little thought to where our decision-making ability comes from. To many, it seems to be an extension of our personalities and opinions. Simply put, we rarely think about *how* we think. Through studies of individuals who have either experienced brain trauma or undergone surgery on different portions of their brain, neuroscientists have known for years that our capacity for cognitive thought comes primarily from what is called the prefrontal cortex of the brain's frontal lobes.[4] It is located at the front of the brain, behind the forehead.

This area is the source of thought that is responsible for setting priorities, organizing plans and ideas, forming strategies, controlling impulses, and allocating attention.[5] This type of thinking is "cognitive," which also includes initiating appropriate and moral behavior, anticipating how behavior today can affect one's future, and sound judgment decisions. The adolescent years are critical for developing these functions. While young people can make some good judgment calls for themselves, it is impossible for them to make fully mature judgment decisions until their mid-twenties, when their brains are finally mature.[6]

One of the best and most understandable evidences of this observation is that car rental companies will not rent their cars to a person under the age of twenty-five unless special arrangements have been made or a higher rate is charged. The reason given by these companies is that the risk of damage and destruction of their property is excessive when driven by younger drivers, regardless of education or employment.

The finding, therefore, that cognitive maturity does not reach completion until the mid-twenties does not mean that young people are somehow physically slow or that they do not possess the capacity for complex thought. It does mean that their brains are not fully physically equipped to make sound judgments and reason through long-term consequences of behavior they might become involved in until a little later in life. When people first hear this information they often take it to mean that young people are inherently less intelligent than adults. This is a misinterpretation—young people can be extremely intelligent. For example, Mozart completed many compositions before the age of fourteen; Picasso painted the *Picador* at age eight; there are many other examples of people demonstrating intelligence and giftedness at a young age. Also, it does not mean that young people are not otherwise physically mature. LeBron James went directly from high school basketball to the NBA at the age of nineteen, a more physically gifted basketball player than many who were years older and far more experienced.

The ability to make sound judgments, then, does not depend on one's intelligence.

What we now know about development of this part of the brain—the prefrontal cortex—is that during the explosive period of adolescent brain development, synapses (the connections that bridge the gaps between neurons) play an integral part in forming the mature brain. Research has shown that there are two periods in one's life during which there is an explosive proliferation of connections between brain cells—during the last few weeks before birth and just before puberty. The brain manufactures far more of these connections (synapses) than are necessary. The interesting thing we now know about this excess of synapses is that some are meant to be strengthened and some are meant to die. It just depends on what we experience.[7] As we have already seen, synapses that strengthen and proliferate are those that are used (think of "use them or lose them"). The synapses that are not used weaken or die.[8]

> "I've seen the changes in some of my friends. I've seen them cry and feel bad and lose hope that they will ever be loved. I haven't found the love of my life yet either, but I am so glad I don't have the baggage they do."
>
> —Cheryl, 26

Setting the course

Adolescent brains can be positively molded by structure, guidance, and discipline provided by caring parents and other adults. This may include any number of positive inputs including loving, caring guidance, discipline (sometimes unpleasant but not dangerous), and also behavior in which the teen is required to take a chance because the outcome is unpredictable: trying out for the high school football team, learning to drive, going to college. These all carry certain emotional or even physical risks, but are necessary in order for the young person to separate from parents and grow into an individual.

Adolescent brains can also be negatively molded by unstructured experiences or bad input such as neglect, poor guidance, poor structure, or lack of discipline. For these unfortunate youth, this means that the guidance they receive and experiences they have come from the media, pop culture, or peers who are as neglected, immature, and poorly guided as they are.

What is certain is that the adolescent brain will be molded by one or the other.[9]

The point here is that if young people are not guided by parents, mentors, and other caring adults, but make their own decisions based on these less than optimal types of bonding, they often make poor decisions.[10] As we explained in chapter 2, this information has many implications. One implication is that, as we have shown, young people can develop early bonding to someone they find attractive. If they feel that "this is the one for them," they can enter into progressive physical contact with that person until they have had sexual intercourse and are then even more closely bonded to the person and "addicted" to having sex.[11] Research has shown that these relationships eventually break apart far more often than they succeed.[12]

An obvious question is that if skin-to-skin or sexual contact causes such bonding, why don't more of these young couples stay together? And the truth is that a few do. We all know examples of very young couples who become pregnant, get married, and stay married for many years.

We also know teenagers who become attached to each other and the relationship drags on for months or even years in spite of one person abusing, cheating on, or degrading the other.

But for the vast majority, these relationships begun while the couple is young and unmarried are short-lived.

The chance of the bonding growing tighter and more permanent, resulting in a lifelong commitment is not realized. These breakups are due to any number of reasons, including attraction to another person, boredom with the current partner, a family move, opinions of peers, the distraction of other activities, even parental disapproval, among countless others. But in spite of the brevity of these sexual encounters, research indicates that bonding does occur, even when a couple has only engaged in sex a single time.[13]

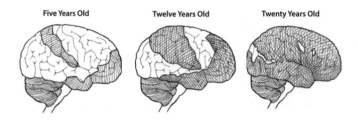

Five Years Old   **Twelve Years Old**   **Twenty Years Old**

The prefrontal cortex of the brain is not mature until a person grows out of adolescence and into their mid-twenties. Shaded portions represent the growing complexity and sophistication of the brain from age five to age twenty. This development is a key factor in an individual's ability to make mature judgment decisions.

Further, there is evidence that when this sex/bonding/breaking-up cycle is repeated a few or many times—even when the bonding was short-lived—damage is done to the important, built-in ability to develop significant and meaningful connection to other human beings.[14]

Another negative consequence is that as young people experience these sexual relationships it affects their brains, molding them not only to damage their attachment ability but to become desensitized to the risk of short-term sexual relationships, eventually believing that this behavior is harmless and acceptable, and does not involve the psychological and mental health part of themselves.[15] In contrast, the relationship that continues long-term experiences a bonding that, in a sense, glues the two people together for life. This bonding, as we have examined, is due in part to the oxytocin and vasopressin secreted into the woman's and man's brains as a result of their contact with each other. This is the deep, abiding love of a mature relationship.[16] One long-term result of the mature love relationship that stays intact (and there are many such positive results, such as providing a stable home environment for child security) is a relaxed, trusting, loving, rewarding, faithful, sexual relationship.[17]

The healthy progression of relationship strengthens the brain cell connections associated with "attachment" of one person to another, helping to ensure the permanence of the relationship that finds its healthiest expression with sexual consummation in marriage.[18]

But this natural process can be short-circuited. During the intense early romantic period a couple wants to be together. This togetherness can obviously include physical closeness. The physical closeness will normally produce sexual interest. If individuals in this early phase of their relationship spend time with intimate skin-to-skin closeness and then become sexually involved, it will activate the oxytocin and vasopressin-induced bonding.[19] Since this bonding has taken place before consideration of issues that could be divisive has occurred, the couple may break up when these very practical considerations intrude, as they always will. Then the breaking of the bond happens, with pain sometimes felt like physical pain, and the regrets occur.[20]

However, when a short-term relationship breaks up—

and certainly when a relationship that is an early intense romantic relationship breaks up—it is felt in the same brain centers that feel physical pain and can actually be seen on brain scans.[21] Like any other powerful experience, an intense romantic relationship molds the mind.

The bonding process can also be short-circuited by a couple progressing immediately to sex. People involved in this behavior either don't think about the risk or believe they can disconnect their sexual involvement from the rest of who they are. We have shown that this is impossible. Thus, unconscious damage also occurs because it violates the integrity of personhood, because anything we do involves the whole person, even if we don't realize it.[22]

Finally, the finding that the brain centers that produce feelings of romance and love are different and separate from the brain centers responsible for lust is a huge warning to adolescents and young adults. A selfish and manipulative person may have an intense desire to have sex with another person. To accomplish that goal, they may lie about being in love. It is important to know the desire someone has for sex can exist without any feelings of caring, love, or romance.[23] This is something that takes some life experience to recognize, which is why even young adults still need guidance.

All this adds up to show that if adults merely provide adolescents with facts about behavior, but don't give them guidance on how to act on this information, teens and young adults cannot make the very best decisions and often will make poor decisions. It is crucial that parents and other influential adults provide adolescents with the guidance to make the best decisions based on the facts that have been presented.

Adolescent judgment, therefore, is in gradual formation and will only achieve true maturity when shepherded by the guidance of parents or committed and caring mentors. As children grow older, the need for adult guidance naturally decreases, and yet continued adult guidance is needed for longer than most of society has realized in past years. The need for advice and supervision extends through the college-age years and for two or three years after.

In addition, the guidance of parents and other caring adults can help structurally develop the brain of a young person, thus enabling her to make the very best decisions by the time she is fully cognitively mature. This guidance allows her to have the best chance of becoming who she is meant to be, the best chance of fulfilling her dreams.[24]

Responsible parents, and those who support them, can help adolescents and young adults avoid risky behavior that can damage them permanently. In fact, recent surveys of college students show that parents influence the decisions they make about sex more than even their friends do.[25]

The Connection Inspection

While the brain and body need to develop to reach their full potential, humans are also born with certain traits built in from birth. These inborn characteristics are sometimes referred to as instinct, and include things such as the ability to understand meaning through facial expressions, or the ability to acquire language. A critical human trait, one that has enormous implications for sex and relationships, is the need to connect to other human beings.[26]

> "We kept having sex even though I knew he was seeing other people. I just needed to be with him, I needed him to hold me. We even did it in his car. It was humiliating, but I didn't know what else to do."
>
> —Samantha, 20

It is a scientifically validated finding that emotionally healthy humans connect to each other. It is felt in the strangest ways. Have you ever wondered why, when another person yawns, you often do too? Have you ever thought about why you feel the pain of someone you love when they are experiencing devastating problems in their lives? Have you wondered why you can almost predict what someone else is going to say before they say it? These and other thoughts, feelings, and actions are evidence of the "connectedness" that is a common, necessary, and normal aspect of human nature. Without this connectedness we would not only be emotionally but physically less healthy. This connectedness comes directly from the way our brains are formed and function from even before birth.

For example, if babies are given adequate nutrition and health care, but are otherwise left in their cribs untouched, they usually do not thrive and can even die.[27] This connectedness is not only something that exists in us as human beings but is there for a purpose—it contributes to our being fully human and to our being able to accomplish those things we are capable of and want to succeed at, not just physically but emotionally, psychologically, relationally, and so on. And as we shall see, it is the very first step in building healthy, meaningful relationships that are vital for a truly fulfilled life.[28]

The human brain is formed so that at birth it demands "connecting" to other human beings. Here is how Allan N. Schore of the UCLA School of Medicine puts it: "We are born to form attachments . . . our brains are physically wired to develop in tandem with another's, through emotional communication, beginning before words are spoken."[29]

Italian neuroscientist Giacomo Rizzolatti discovered a certain kind of brain cells, "mirror neurons," that help explain aspects of our connectedness to others. These neurons are responsible for allowing us to feel a loved one's pain, or experience hunger when we hear someone bite into an apple. Mirror neurons also appear to be essential to the way children learn.[30]

In addition, psychologist Daniel Goleman explains that "imitative learning has long been recognized as a major avenue of childhood development. But findings about mirror neurons explain how children can gain mastery simply from watching. As they watch, they are etching in their own brains a repertoire for emotion, for behavior, and for how the world works."[31]

This process is critical from birth, when babies bond and learn from their mothers, all the way throughout childhood and adolescence. It serves as further proof that humans are profoundly social beings, who possess an inborn need to connect and bond with others.[32]

"She wanted to do it—I didn't push her or anything. But when it was over she cried and acted like it was a big mistake. I wish it hadn't happened. But we can't take it back and now everything is messed up."

—Andy, 15

Connectedness, for the average, healthy person, is a part of who we are and how we function. It is wired into our brains when we are still in our mother's womb. This connectedness is passed on by our genes and is necessary for us to survive and thrive as healthy, capable persons. If we have mothers who are highly nurturing, we develop better connectedness and we ourselves are more likely to nurture our own children better and help them connect better with others.[33]

The sex connection

It is probably obvious by now what the natural and healthy inclination for connectedness has to do with sex. Studies show that the primary desire of adolescent girls in romantic relationships is intimacy. When a survey published in *Seventeen* magazine queried thousands of teen readers on sexual issues, fully 40 percent of participating teens reported that they had assured a potential love interest that they would consent to just a "hook-up" when what they really wanted was a relationship.[34] In short, sex is an intense experience of connectedness. As we have noted, when people have sex, the act triggers the release of dopamine in their brains, thus rewarding them for engaging in such an exciting and pleasurable act.

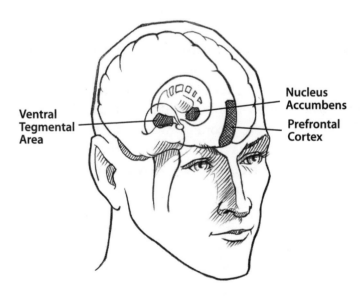

Brain areas most commonly involved in mature or long-lasting and committed love.

As we've discussed, oxytocin is released in the female as this behavior persists, bonding her to her sexual partner and creating a greater desire to repeat the activity with him. When a male engages in sex, vasopressin is released, bonding him to his partner and also stimulating the desire for more sex. Most important, the synapses that govern decisions about sex in both the male and female brains are strengthened in ways that make it easier to choose to have sex in the future, while synapses that govern sexual restraint are weakened and deteriorate. In short, engaging in sex creates a chain reaction of brain activities that lead to the desire for more sex and greater levels of attachment between two people.

It may sound blunt, but if we try to eliminate this connectedness from sex, we remove the uniquely human aspect of it, and the sexual act becomes nothing more than raw animal behavior. However, when this connectedness is allowed to mature in the context of a lifelong committed relationship, sex is a wonderful, sustaining expression of love.

Obviously, individuals do not carry the connectedness they have in infancy directly into adulthood, knowing exactly which person to connect with in a lifelong, mutually faithful monogamous relationship. There are some interim steps, as even a cursory observation will note. However, there are stages of emotional development leading to that point:

- *Infatuation or nascent love:* this is the emergence of interest in the opposite sex during adolescence. An adolescent may have very emotional and strongly felt "love" for one individual and a few months later, a similar strong feeling for another person.[35]

At this point, several divergent paths emerge. This is a critical juncture, where most people choose to engage in one of the following patterns of behavior:

- *Short-term sexual relationships:* these are sexual relationships that have very little connectedness and, according to extensive research, the least satisfying sex. The normal connecting and bonding seems to become damaged by such relationships, often leading to a pattern of serial sex that can last for years.[36]
- *Long-term monogamy outside of marriage:* a sexual relationship that usually results in weaker connectedness, less permanent relationships, sex with somewhat less satisfaction and bonding.[37]
- *Love:* this is the real thing and causes a couple to view each other as potential lifelong mates (or at least long-term mates). This emotion often occurs in young adulthood after the cognitive development of adolescence is largely completed. Though this relationship may not invariably lead to marriage, it often does.[38]
- *Marriage:* this is the sexual relationship in which connectedness is found to be the most long-lasting and strong and the relationship associated with sex in which the greatest satisfaction, bonding, and healthy sexual addiction is found.[39]

Love? or infatuation?

What can we possibly learn from neuroscience about something so indefinable and personal as love? As it turns out, we can learn a lot. What we learn can help us understand our own feelings and can also help us give guidance to our young people as they deal with the powerful emo-

> "I feel like I can't trust anyone anymore. I thought he cared for me, but now I wonder if it was just all about sex for him. I don't really know how to know the difference."
>
> —Chandra, 16

tion they often call love. But is it really?

Infatuation refers to the incredibly exciting awakening of sexual awareness embodied in focus on a person of the opposite sex. However, infatuation does not befall just preteens and young teens. It can "hit" anyone of any age. We call infatuation the great imitator of true love because it appears that the same brain centers that signal "passionate new love" to an individual are the ones that cause a more immature feeling, that of "infatuation." It is therefore impossible from brain study techniques as well as by social study techniques to say whether the feelings one has for another person constitute infatuation or legitimate early love.[40]

Since not even a study of the brain can tell the difference between true love and infatuation, parents as well as young people themselves should be cautious when an adolescent pronounces himself "in love." This feeling of love can be very intense, similar to obsessive-compulsive disorder, causing people to think of doing things they would not ordinarily do.[41] This intense emotional state may last several months. (There is no specific cutoff time found by scientists.) This cutoff is not sudden and may in part be due to a gradual decline in the level of dopamine.[42]

Many couples break up during this time for any number of reasons, such as other priorities (education or job), lack of common interests, personality problems, disagreements over goals, religion, and so on. Some of the reasons people break up are difficult to define. They might be included under the term *intuition*. One or the other or both "just know" the relationship, as intense and exciting as it is, is not right in the long run.[43]

Having this information at hand, it is easy to see the advantages of patiently letting a relationship mature before committing to it through sexual involvement. Letting a relationship mature means taking time. Even though brain scans cannot tell whether initial infatuation will become true love or not, they can show the difference between the early passionate stage of romantic love and that of long-term, comfortable, and relaxed, loving attachment.[44]

One reason it is best to not become involved sexually before marriage is that statistics say that a relationship started prior to the age of twenty-one will probably not be permanent. As any adult can attest, infatuation is usually short-lived, lasting only weeks or months and not years as does true love. Statistics show that if young people begin having sex when they are sixteen years old, more than 44 percent of them will have had five or more sexual partners by the time they are in their twenties. If they are older than twenty when they initiate sex, only 15 percent will have had more than five sexual partners, while just over 50 percent will have committed sexually to only one partner.[45]

> *It is easy to see the advantages of patiently letting a relationship mature before committing to it through sexual involvement.*

If people of any age become sexually involved before marriage, the intensity of the desire for repetition of sexual activity can overwhelm everything else in the relationship. Sex at this immature stage can keep a person from honestly evaluating the other person. Sex can make a person feel that the other person is the "right one" because the bonding and dopamine high it brings can blind one to honestly looking at the other's faults and lack of compatibility.[46]

Hooked on love

> "We're proud of it. We set a goal to be pure for each other on our wedding day and we did it. It wasn't easy, but it taught us a lot about each other. I'm glad we did it."
>
> —David, 30

We have seen how experience produces brain molding, both in positive and in negative manners. This process is also powerfully at work in sustained romantic relationships. As these intense and exciting relationships develop, they cause connections between brain cells to grow stronger and more numerous. As we know, when those connections grow and cause more pleasurable behavioral experiences, more dopamine is released. This abundant outpouring of dopamine is similar to what happens in other more commonly recognized forms of addiction such as substance abuse. "Drugs such as cocaine and amphetamine target dopamine neurons."[47]

In other words, love, on a biochemical level, is a lot like addiction. The healthy addiction of a lifelong monogomous sexual relationship even has measurable physical benefits. Consider what these researchers found:

> Janice K. Kiecolt-Glaser and her colleagues at the Ohio State University Medical Center conducted a series of studies examining the connections between close sexual relationships, especially those of married couples, and physiological processes such as immune, endocrine, and cardiovascular functioning. These re-

searchers report growing evidence linking relationship intimacy to better health, including stronger immune systems and physical wounds taking less time to heal. Conversely, high-conflict (anti-intimate) marital relationships appear to weaken the immune system and increase vulnerability to disease, especially among women, including worsening the body's response to proven vaccines and lengthening the amount of time required for physical wounds to heal.[48]

In short, brain researchers and other scientists are now clearly mapping out what might be called the biochemistry of connection.[49]

Other research has revealed numerous benefits of individuals maintaining long-term connectedness to their mate. James Coan, in a study titled "Lending a Hand: Social Regulation of the Neural Response to Threat" gave a mild electrical shock to married individuals. If they were holding the hands of their mate, their ability to handle the shock was much better than if sitting apart. While the physical contact made no difference in the way it felt to be shocked, individuals being comforted by their spouse were reassured and calmed.[50] This is just a small example of how connectedness with a spouse is even found to be associated with better health.

Love, Romance, and . . . Lust?

One of the most startling findings of all in this brain research about love and lust is that they are each handled distinctly differently by the brain. Recent studies[51] showed certain brain centers to light up in subjects as a result of being shown pictures of their beloved. These patterns of

brain activity were distinctly different from the brain activity associated with lust as shown by other experiments.[52]

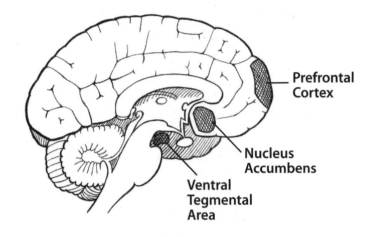

Side view of brain areas most commonly involved in mature love.

This means of course that a man (or woman) can be
sexually attracted to another person, approach that person
for sex, engage in sex, and yet have no sincerely love-moti-
vated thought or interest at all because all their desire arises
from the brain's center for "lust." Young men and women
especially need to be aware of and alert to their own feelings and to those of a potential partner. A person might approach another with a show of warmth and consideration,
acts of kindness, even with words of love and commitment.
But all this can be based on lust—a counterfeit emotion designed to manipulate the other into having sex, with no romantic or love interest at all.

While it is normal and not wrong for a human being to
have lustful sexual urges—and lust in the context of a loving married relationship is certainly normal—it is the acting on lustful urges alone that is out of sync with human

nature. This is critical to understand if we are to be emotionally healthy, and an understanding that is necessary for a future that is as free of problems as possible. To practice sex out of sync is to ignore the fact that healthy human behavior demands the integration of all of what we are—body, mind, emotions, and spirit.[53]

Sex practiced inappropriately can both control and damage the relationship. As one writer puts it, a nonmarital "relationship is only as old as it is nonsexual. The relationship stops growing once it becomes sexual, because the erotic aspect will become the primary focus of [the couple's] time together."[54] Not only is such a relationship damaged, but the two people involved can also be.

On the other hand, in a relationship of true love and long-term commitment, sex takes its appropriate place—not at the center of the relationship, but as one of the natural outcomes of the healthy connectedness of two people. Sex will then be a catalyst to the full, healthy, long-term committed relationship it strengthens.

These are the things that define us as human. True "love" includes applying this mature thought process to another in the context of romance, attachment, and bonding. Allowing such love to develop and then to guide us will lead to healthy and good decisions about behavior. Such decisions will then expand our horizons, help eliminate baggage that might weigh us down, and send us into true, life-fulfilling love.

to THINK ABOUT

- ◆ For how long does a person's brain remain moldable? What are some ways to positively and negatively mold the developing brain?

- ◆ What happens to the brain of a person who repeats the sex/bonding/breaking-up cycle?

- ◆ The authors tell us "it is a scientifically validated finding that emotionally healthy humans connect to each other." In what ways do humans connect with one another, scientifically speaking?

WE HUMANS HAVE A BUILT-IN DESIRE for attachment. When we exercise the choices that tie us to others we are at our most human.

Chapter Four

BAGGAGE CLAIM

"There are so many things I want to accomplish in life. Having a child at fifteen is not one of them."

—Sharon, 15

Almost everyone has sex at some point in their lives.

Whether it's in high school, on a honeymoon with their soul mate, or on a one-night stand, nearly every adult (and a majority of people reading this book) has experienced sex. Unfortunately, not everyone chooses when or how they will experience sex. Many people have fallen victim to molestation during childhood or were manipulated or misled as a teenager.[1] Still more people chose to have sex, but later regretted it when the relationship ended or they contracted an illness from their partner.[2]

As we have seen, sex is far more complicated than just a momentary physical act of pleasure—engaging in sex almost always carries long-term psychological consequences, either life-enhancing or life-limiting. The brain chemical effect of sex has happened, in varying degrees, to everyone who has experienced sexual intercourse. Does this mean that individuals who engaged in casual sex even once are somehow "broken" and cannot be fixed? What about people who have had multiple partners, or lost their virginity at

an early age? What about rape victims who had no choice
in the matter and are left scarred by a violent sexual experience?

While important work has been done to understand
and treat the emotional scars of rape and sexual abuse, more
could be accomplished with a broader understanding of
how the sex act triggers the release of brain chemicals, setting off a chain reaction with profound consequences.
Rather than acknowledging that sex has an impact on a person's entire being—both mental and physical, good and also
sometimes bad—many choose to ignore the evidence.

In the interest of tolerance and acceptance and a modern view of what is supposedly "good and right and natural" for young people, modern society has normalized
individuals involved in sexual activity outside the boundaries of a lifelong relationship.[3] The feelings of shame and
regret, not to mention physical repercussions, for such behavior has been minimized or attributed to other factors by
those who say that it is acceptable for adolescents to engage
in sexual activity when they feel they are ready. When
young people do experience unfortunate problems from sex,
the very same young people are blamed for their mistakes.
Such blame takes multiple forms, such as "they just didn't
use their condoms consistently enough" or "they thought
they were emotionally mature enough but they weren't" or
"the sex they had was not appropriately consensual on the
part of both persons."[4]

The Drive for More

Sexual intercourse *is* a normal behavior for human beings. Without a sex drive, the human race would become
extinct. Therefore, the body naturally seeks out and engages
in sex as a built-in survival mechanism to ensure the sur-

> "Sex just seemed like part of the date and usually took place by the second time I went out with someone. It left me feeling empty, but I figured that's the way things were. I felt lonely and hollow inside."
>
> —Laney, 26

vival of the human race. The cascade of hormonal events that occur in the body and brain as a result of sexual involvement are normal events and happen independently of age (once puberty is achieved and considering some decline in older age), marital status, social status, ethnic makeup, education, and so on. These brain chemical reflexes are built into the body and are put there for good reason. For example, as we have examined, the dopamine reward that follows sexual behavior causes an individual to desire sex again and again once they have experienced it. Since pregnancy occurs only 25 percent of the time with one act of sex at the time of ovulation even in the most fertile women, it takes repeated sexual encounters to assure the greatest opportunity for pregnancy to occur.[5] Because survival of the human race is dependent on this occurring, the desire for sex to ensure pregnancy is built into the human body, with dopamine and other hormones at work to assure that the man and woman keep trying.

Statistics, research, and casual observation tell us that many people are responding to these natural urges outside of the context of marriage or monogamous relationships. Forty-six percent of all high school students (freshmen through seniors) have had sexual intercourse.[6] Approximately 75 percent of graduating high school students have had sex.[7] Nearly half of all college students report having oral sex one or more times in the past 30 days.[8] Almost none of these students are seriously committed to their partners for the long term.[9]

We have already seen that the earlier an individual ini-
tiates sexual intercourse, the more likely it is that they will
have multiple sexual partners. A study by the Centers for
Disease Control and Prevention showed that if girls were
younger than sixteen years of age at their first sexual experience, 58.1 percent of them would later report more than
five sexual partners when interviewed in their late twenties. Only a little more than 10 percent had limited their
sexual experiences to only one partner. However, if they
were over twenty years of age at first intercourse, only 15.2
percent had more than five sexual partners over the next
few years, but a significant 52.2 percent had limited to only
one sexual partner.[10]

Another study had similar findings. It showed that adolescent females who begin sexual activity at age 15–19 years
will have, on average, more than seven voluntary sexual
partners during their lives. In contrast, females who maintain their virginity until age twenty-one will have, on average, two sexual partners during their lives. Data also shows
that delay of sexual intercourse for males also significantly
reduces the number of lifetime partners.[11]

It seems that the dopamine reward signal is working
very well in these young people. Once they experience sex,
they want to repeat it again and again. We have discussed
elsewhere how sex is similar to drug, alcohol, or nicotine
addiction; it is understandable that a young (or older) person would want to experience that same rush again.[12]

It is helpful to note that when individuals in a relationship break up and they then enter another relationship,
they will tend to move quickly and prematurely to the same
degree of intimacy in the new relationship that they experienced in the old one, even with partners with dissimilar
intimacy patterns. In other words, if a couple has been hav-

ing intercourse as a part of their relationship and then break up, each, on entering a relationship with another person, will tend to move quickly to sexual intercourse with the new partner, even if the new partner has not had sexual intercourse before.[13] The dopamine reward for sex is strong.

The Pain of Broken Bonds

As we have emphasized throughout this book, every time a person has sexual intercourse or intimate physical contact, bonding takes place.[14] Whenever breakups occur in bonded relationships there is confusion and often pain in the brains of the young people involved because the bond has been broken.[15]

When two people join physically, powerful neurohormones are released because of the sexual experience, making an impression on the synapses in their brains and hardwiring their bond. When they stay together for life, their bonding matures. This is a major factor that keeps them together, providing desire for intercourse, resulting in offspring, and assuring those offspring of a nurturing two-parent home in which to grow.[16]

The longer people are together, the stronger their bond can become. When that bond is broken, more damage is done than simply the loss of the relationship. The neurochemical imprint of that sexual experience remains, often for many years, impeding the very bonding process that leads to future healthy relationships. This pattern severely damages one of the most important abilities humans are

> "To be honest, I just want to get it over with. I'm scared about how it will feel and what it means. But I love him and I'm afraid he will leave me if we don't take the next step."
>
> —Keisha, 15

born with, the ability to bond to another person.[17] This bonding ability resides in some of the deepest and most fundamental parts of the human brain, and when damaged may require years of counseling for even the most committed person to heal.

On its most basic level, it seems that young people feel that something very important to themselves has been damaged by these sexual relationships that are so temporary. Perhaps they feel that their ability to connect or bond to others is in danger. Because the ability to connect, as we have seen, is so vital to our being emotionally healthy functioning human beings, these young people intuitively sense that something is desperately wrong, though they may have trouble articulating what it is. These disturbed impressions may lead to depression and even suicidal thoughts.

We should not be surprised at these stark statements. In chapter 1 we looked at some of the statistics that demonstrate these impressions, but the information bears repeating here. In a study that controlled for other mitigating factors, sexually active teen girls were shown to be three times as likely to report that they are depressed all, most of, or a lot of the time as compared to girls who are still abstinent. Sexually active boys are more than twice as likely to report depression as boys who are still abstinent. Sexually active girls are three times as likely as nonsexually active girls to have attempted suicide, while sexually active boys are seven times as likely as non-sexually active boys to have attempted suicide.[18]

The Spring 2006 American College Health Association Survey reported that 38 percent of male students and 47 percent of female students felt so depressed during the previous year that it was sometimes hard for them to function. Almost as telling was the finding of the same report that

54.6 percent of male students and 66.7 percent of female students felt that "things were hopeless" at some point in the past year. Also, approximately 10 percent of students reported seriously considering attempting suicide at least once during the previous year (8.4 percent of males and 9.8 percent of females) and approximately 1.3 percent had actually attempted suicide in the past year.[19] This and other studies seem to indicate that some of this psychological stress, depression, and suicide ideation is due to the sexual involvement of these young people.[20] Exactly how much is unclear according to the available data, though some of it is due to the short-term nature of such relationships.[21] Additionally, adolescents who learn they are infected with an STD (and one in four sexually active adolescents is newly infected with an STD each year) suffer from depression at much higher rates than those who are not affected.[22]

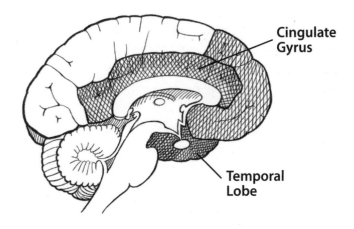

The locations of the brain believed to be most involved with depression.

Several years ago during the course of a routine exam, a thirty-five-year-old Texas woman was asked about her history of sexual activity. She specifically remembered her first experience, and related how painful it was. She confided that she had never enjoyed sex and in fact had "hated every minute of it." She described negative thoughts and bad memories of sexual experiences that came back to her while in the shower or in bed. To her, sexual activity is "something that literally stays with a person for an entire lifetime."[23]

Becoming sexually active and having multiple sexual partners can damage an individual's ability to develop healthy, mature, and long-lasting relationships. This seems to especially hold true for a future healthy and stable marriage. Several studies show an association between sex before marriage and a higher divorce rate when those individuals eventually marry.[24] This would suggest, among other things, that the person's ability to bond as husband or wife is damaged, causing that couple to struggle with the commitment that comes with marriage.

The encouraging news is that studies clearly show that this does not *always* happen. However, a couple who has had sex before marriage, particularly those who have had sex with someone other than their eventual wife or husband, should not wait but very soon confront the issue even if it involves counseling if they begin seeing fractures in their relationship. If they do not do this they may be at increased risk for unhappiness in marriage or even divorce.[25]

Collateral Damage

Although this book is primarily about the third risk— the effects of sex on the brain—we would be remiss not to touch on the other two risks as well. STDs and unwanted

"We know we shouldn't really have sex, so we just do oral stuff. That way everyone stays safe from diseases and no one gets in trouble."

—Michael, 18

pregnancies are part of the greater discussion, since they also affect people's mental and emotional states. In addition to the brain chemical effects of sex that have already been discussed, bodily fluids and secretions are exchanged between partners during sexual contact. The exchange occurs not only during intercourse, but also during other activities such as oral sex. If a person has a sexually transmitted infection, some of the germs of that infection are in the person's bodily fluids. Those germs can then infect their partner with herpes, gonorrhea, even HPV, or other diseases one of them might be infected with.

Today, more than 70 million Americans are living with some form of sexually transmitted infection.[26] Each year, a whopping 19 million new cases are contracted. Half of these are in people under the age of twenty-five.[27]

While much work remains to be done in educating the public about sexually transmitted infections, it is evident that the physical dangers of sex with multiple partners is far more widely acknowledged than the psychological and emotional dangers this book is about.[28] Therefore, the debate over safer sex, condom use, sex education in schools, and national health policy are best left for another venue. The purposes of this book is to demonstrate new neuroscientific research—a wealth of new data suggesting that sex involves the entire person, physically, mentally, emotionally, and in every other way. The physical ramifications of nonmarital sex should not be ignored (STIs and nonmarital pregnancy) and neither should the emotional effects.

But the emotional effect is not just a feeling, but arises from the way one's brain is molded or is damaged by unfortunate experiences.

For example, consider the young woman at a clinic in Mississippi who was informed that she had herpes, a sexually transmitted infection that causes outbreaks of painful blisters in the genital area. There is no cure for the condition—simply a regimen of treatment that works to prevent or minimize future outbreaks. Shocked and dismayed, the young patient reacted with tears and angry denial. After the initial surprise had subsided, her doctor began to discuss transmission—how she acquired it, from whom, and when. Eventually, the conversation turned to the possibility of her having sex in the future. "If I did," she said, "I would not be able to tell anyone that I had herpes." Her shame and regret was so great, she claimed she would be willing to endanger another person rather than face the consequences of an open and honest disclosure of her infection. Sadly, this scenario plays out in the lives of people across the country every day.[29]

Similarly, out-of-wedlock pregnancy has a dramatic impact on the course of life for the mother, the father, and the unborn child. Unmarried teen mothers are more likely to drop out of school, receive welfare, have mental and physical health problems, continue to have out-of-wedlock pregnancies, and even if they subsequently marry are more likely to divorce.[30] For example, less than two-thirds of teen mothers graduate from high school or earn a GED within two years of giving birth.[31] Here are more specifics:

- 80 percent of unwed fathers don't marry the teen mother of their baby;[32]

- 80 percent of unwed teen mothers eventually receive welfare;[33]
- 50 percent of all single mothers on welfare were teenagers when they had their first baby;[34]
- 70 percent of unwed mothers receive no financial support from the fathers of their children;[35]
- Teen mothers receive an average of $67 per month in child support;[36]
- Nearly one-half of all teen pregnancies under the age of 19 occur in relationships with males more than three years older.[37]

These startling statistics are no secret. That's why there have been enormous efforts to encourage contraceptive use by sexually active teenagers. A health-care provider may consider this appropriate, but should only entertain such an option if provided with intense, one-on-one counseling and not given as an open-ended prescription, but as a stop-gap until the adolescent returns to abstinence, a change in behavior much more common than conventional wisdom would indicate.[38] However, when statistics gathered during all these years of emphasis on contraceptive use are viewed objectively, we understand the importance of changing the emphasis to helping young people and older single individuals consider their behavior and not just consider how to avoid an unplanned pregnancy. To ignore the facts that have now been gathered during years of contraceptive/condom emphasis is to put one's head in the sand and leave other young people at risk to nonmarital pregnancy. For example:

- 20 percent of those aged 12–18 using the birth-control pill get pregnant within six months;[39]

- 20 percent of teens younger than 18 using condoms get pregnant within one year;[40]
- 8 percent of adult women using oral contraceptives become pregnant each year;[41]
- 32 percent of women discontinue oral contraceptive use after one year;[42]
- 50 percent of female teens using contraception and cohabiting with a boyfriend get pregnant within a year.[43]

Adolescent brain molding often results in young people who have developed a pattern of sexual activity to often continue that activity.[44] This activity will, regardless of contraceptive or condom use, often lead to pregnancy. Pregnancy for the unmarried girl, for the father, if he is a teenager, and for the child that results can have lifelong consequences. It often results in none of the three primary people involved ever achieving their hopes or dreams or achieving their potential. And of course, condoms and contraceptives provide no protection from the influences of sex on the brain.

> "I was so drunk the first time that I don't really remember it. But now that my virginity is gone, it doesn't make any sense not to have sex. I've already done it, so I might as well have fun."
>
> —Susan, 19

I Had No Choice

Rape and sexual coercion are the most extreme forms of unhealthy sexual behavior. They are violent acts of aggression against the victim. Unfortunately, these tragedies are very common. However, we can learn a great deal about the impact of sex on an individual when we explore this problem.

- 30 percent of women of all
  ages report that the first sex they experienced was
  not voluntary.[45]
- More than 40 percent of girls who first experience
  sex under the age of 15 describe it as involuntary or
  unwanted.[46]
- The Centers for Disease Control and Prevention
  found that 20 percent of college women had been
  forced to have sex against their will at some time
  during their lives.[47]

A recent study of the brain-derived neurotrophic factor, labeled BDNF,[48] gives us major insight into what happens in the brains of many of these victims. The research, done at the University of Texas Southwestern Medical School in Dallas, Texas, revealed that traumatic intimidation leads to high levels of stress that can cause the release of excessive levels of BDNF from the frontal lobes of the brain. If BDNF levels get too high, genes in the frontal lobe of the brain are turned on, resulting in social withdrawal and depression. The researchers believed that abuse and violence lead to excessive production of BDNF. As a result, the individual will experience depression, withdrawal from society, fearful behavior to any threat, a tendency to addictive behaviors, and an inability to enjoy intimacy in the future.

Discussing BDNF brings up a more subtle question about a less traumaticexperience than rape. Will a woman or man who is involved in sex with someone they feel is just using them as a sex object, or having repeated broken sexual relationships, continue to bond with and trust their sexual partners? Probably not. And this crushing of these inborn healthy responses to sex may be one of the saddest outcomes of such sexual experiences—for damaging an individual's future enjoyment of sex and bonding with a partner who loves and cherishes them.

A study on women in college offers confirmation for this research. The study showed that when compared to women who had not been date-raped, the date-raped women had lower self-esteem and lower scores on adaptiveness and self-control.[49]

The term "post-traumatic stress disorder" describes the condition that results from these and other traumatic experiences. Research has shown that adolescents are uniquely vulnerable to the impact of stress and this is exactly the time when rape, date rape, and sexual coercion are most likely to happen.[50]

In addition to emotional problems, young women who have been sexually abused often experience physical problems such as chronic pelvic pain, chronic abdominal pain, premenstrual syndrome, vaginal discharge, sexually transmitted infections, and nonmarital pregnancies.[51]

Also, sexual abuse sufferers are at risk for re-victimization, or the experience of another attack. Two-thirds of adult rape victims report that they experienced childhood sexual abuse. This surprising correlation must be due in part to brain molding that results from the intense and damaging experience of childhood abuse.[52]

It is likely that being sexually abused can interfere with a male's normal development in his awakening interest in sex. Stepping away from our focus on women and girls (though much of what we have said can be applied directly to boys who have been sexually abused), it is worth mentioning that almost 10 percent of boys who report being sexually abused as children grow up to become pedophiles themselves. Igor Galynaker, a psychiatrist at Beth Israel Medical Center in New York City, has performed brain scans on a number of pedophiles and has found subnormal activity in the temporal lobes. This indicates an abnormally low ability to make sound judgments and consider consequences for actions.[53] Other studies confirm these findings. Vernon Quinsey, a psychologist at Queen's University in Canada speculates that a boy's temporal lobe goes through a transformation as a boy's interest in sex develops during puberty.[54] Perhaps the experience of being molested derails or forestalls that transformation in some way.

While sexual abuse is not the norm for the majority of individuals we can still learn some important lessons from the experiences of those who have faced that tragedy. Among those lessons are the following:

- The impact of sex on the brain can be long-lasting;
- The impact of sex can affect future health and behavior in ways we would never expect unless forewarned; and
- Whether sex is forced, consensual, a one-night stand, or in a healthy marriage, its impact is significant and remarkable.

> "That's how you get a boyfriend. No one will go out with me unless they think I will go all the way. I don't want to be alone. So I have to do it."
>
> —Amanda, 14

Once again we can infer that past experiences guide the development of the brain in these unfortunate situations in an unhealthy way, which then results in future unhealthy behavior.

Mind Games

In addition to rape, unwanted sex often occurs in cases of sexual manipulation. These are instances in which individuals willfully mislead or employ deceptive tactics to trick or entice others into sex in ways that cannot legally be called rape but yet verge on rape. It is helpful to mention a newsworthy event that took place some years ago to put this issue in perspective.

In 1993, a small group of high school boys in the LA suburb of Lakewood, California, formed a group whose stated goal was to see which guy could manipulate the most girls into having sex. These young men were clean-cut, athletically and academically gifted, and seemed destined for successful lives. They called themselves the Spur Posse, named in honor of their basketball heroes, the San Antonio Spurs. Teenage boys in search of casual sex is unfortunate but not unusual. What is unusual is the level of attention this incident received when the group's true aim was revealed after seven girls filed formal complaints. The resulting press coverage and community reaction reveals much about sexual manipulation and the type of messages young people are receiving from our sex-saturated society.

In an interview with *Time* magazine,[55] one of the boys said, "My dad used to brag to his friends. All the dads did. When we brought home girls they liked, they'd say, 'Cool,' and tell their buddies." These boys were confused and dismayed at the public outcry because they had never technically raped a girl and they always used condoms—yet they were subject to severe criticism.

The truth is that they had been abiding by the rules they had been told, or at least that most young people are told in comprehensive sex education classes. These rules and ideas include that they will inevitably have sex, that there must be mutual consent, and that it must be done with condoms. They did not break any of these rules, yet they still were not acting in the best interests of the young women they manipulated into sexual intercourse.

Just because sexual intercourse is not technically rape or forced, it is not necessarily truly and fully consensual or appropriate, especially for younger boys and girls. Without proper guidance, adolescent males often misunderstand or choose to ignore anything short of a flat refusal to becoming more physical in a relationship. A study of self-confessed date rapists found that every instance of sexual coercion followed mutually consensual sex play; the rapists simply ignored the woman's protests about going further.[56] This lack of perception in the minds of teenage boys, willful or otherwise, may explain some of the problems we see encountered by teenage girls who have engaged in sex, especially at younger ages.

Another warning sign for parents and mentors to watch for in young people is involvement in risky behavior such as alcohol, marijuana, or tobacco abuse. Adolescents involved in these behaviors are more likely to initiate sex early and to have an increased number of sexual partners.[57]

The adolescent and young adult brain is far from its final, fully formed state.

It may be that the innate human desire for meaningful connections that all people have cause many young men and women to become involved in casual sexual behavior. Without adult guidance, their natural desire for connectedness and an equally natural interest in sex will often lead to bad decisions. The National Campaign to Prevent Teen Pregnancy has conducted national surveys of youth in the United States for years. They consistently find that high majorities of teens who had become sexually active wish they had waited until they were older to initiate sexual activity. This same organization in a survey found that 93 percent of teenagers think that young people ought to receive a strong abstinence message. This obviously includes teenagers who have had sex (since almost half of the teens in high schools across the country have had sexual intercourse).[58]

The problems young people have experienced with voluntary sex may not be as immediate, obvious, or violent as the problems of rape or coerced sex, but they are nonetheless very real and quite prevalent.

> "It was the hardest thing we ever did, but we are so glad we waited. We had to talk through our disagreements. We couldn't just feel close by having sex—we had to really work things out."
>
> —Charles, 28

Hope for the Future

The adolescent and young adult brain is far from its final, fully formed state. Because it does not reach full cognitive maturity until the mid-twenties, it lacks the brain circuits necessary to make the best behavior decisions, the decisions that will help the individual be as free as possible of baggage from the past that can prevent the individual from achieving his or her potential.

As we have seen, the ideal situation is a home in which the child has two married, biological parents.[59] Any other situation is less ideal, though it does not sentence the child to a compromised life. It just makes it harder for him or her to achieve full potential. Fortunately, there are many, many hardworking single parents with extended families and with mentors to help, and many remarkably successful people come from such environments.

Humans have a built-in desire for attachment. When

we exercise the choices that tie us to others we are at our most human. However, because of immaturity, poorly directed peers, the pressure of society, the attraction of sex to which they are prematurely exposed, abuse, and a myriad of other factors, young people can become involved in behavior patterns that are destructive. These unfortunate experiences can pattern the brain to make the young person repeat destructive behavior and suffer lifelong consequences often impairing hope of achieving their life dreams and goals even if they were born with the gifts and potential of achieving them.

Children, adolescents, and young adults need guidance to make good decisions. This guidance needs to continue, though more indirectly, into the mid-twenties. When the young person receives and wisely heeds this appropriate guidance, his or her brain is actually being molded to almost habitually make behavior decisions that will facilitate their dreams and desires.

to THINK ABOUT

- ◆ Why does the cycle of short-term sexual activity with different partners tend to repeat itself?
- ◆ What are some consequences of inadvisable sexual activity?
- ◆ Sex is just one aspect of personhood. What are others? Why can't sex be separated from what it means to be a person?

WE HAVE A RESPONSIBILITY TO
ourselves to discover our purpose and
live it out. Understanding this should
encourage us, if we want to reach our
fullest potential, to do things that are
stretching, difficult, challenging, and
may even seem unnatural.

Chapter Five

THINKING LONG-TERM

> "I didn't know how to be in a relationship and not have sex. That was how I kept men interested, how I kept them with me. It's why they liked me. Or at least that's what I thought."
>
> —Amy, 25

The material presented so far in this book is certainly sobering, isn't it?

We've learned why it is best to refrain from sexual activity until a person is in a lifelong relationship, something that usually happens only in marriage. We know that many get derailed from the best life they can have by making decisions they look back on with the realization that they hadn't used the best judgment. In this chapter we'll review some of the poor choices people make and why these are not healthy ones. But we'll also talk about why, if a person has made less than optimal choices in the past, that doesn't mean it's the end of the story, because our complex and amazing brain is a moldable structure.

Many people in our society today choose to have sex outside of a lifelong committed relationship. They do this for countless reasons, justifying and rationalizing it according to their own unique circumstances—*he really cares about me,*

*she said she wanted to, we don't want to wait, I was curious
about what it felt like, I was tired of being a virgin, I just wanted
to get it over with,* and so on. Most believe that they have special, unique, justifiable reasons for their behavior. Despite
their many differences, all of these people have at least one
thing in common: they cannot predict the future. No one
knows for certain how a relationship will work out. While
it's *possible* that a couple having sex before marriage will one
day make a lifelong commitment, it is statistically more likely
they won't.[1] In fact, as we have seen, the likeliest outcome of
premarital sex is simply more premarital sex.[2]

Individuals who wait to have sex until marriage have
increased assurance about the success and quality of their
marriage. Most marriages are faithful,[3] most sex in marriage
is good,[4] and most people who don't have sex until marriage
have more stability and more
success in their lives as measured by education, economics,
and emotional stability.[5]

> Life is difficult enough
> without the added
> challenges discussed on
> these pages.

This is not to say that anyone is condemned to a second-
rate life if they've had sex
before marriage. However, research clearly indicates that
doing so means taking some very serious chances. And as
we have seen, it means risking much more than a sexually
transmitted disease or pregnancy. We now know that there
is a further risk—the danger of molding your mind in a way
that makes it more difficult in the future to experience the
joys of a bonded, loving relationship.[6] Our goal in this book
has been to provide data that shows there is more risk with
some choices than with others. This data can inform people
as they make choices so, if they desire, they can choose the

behavior that offers themselves the least present or future problems. Still, some will make the choice to engage in sex with multiple partners despite the abundance of data that refutes the wisdom of such a decision.

Life is difficult enough without the added challenges discussed on these pages. An individual who is forewarned about the consequences of a decision or behavior and acts to avoid it can perhaps pave the way to a better life in the future. This information is not offered as a moral statement. Rather, the information offered here is clearly based on the data that supports the fact that there is a third risk involved in sexual activity—and that sex within the context of a marriage is the ideal behavior for avoiding problems.

Still, some information presented here does not mean that individuals who ignore it or who are faced with sexual situations through no fault of their own are destined to a life of failure and unhappiness. Clearly, even an individual who makes the very best choices can still face sexually related problems such as rape, molestation, or other situations.

However, the odds of persons leading fulfilled and successful lives are greatly increased by practicing sex within the healthiest context.

Living Together: Just another choice?

> "Of course, you should try on shoes before you buy them."
>
> "Naturally, you'll test-drive a car, before you invest in it."
>
> "Certainly, you and your significant other should live together before marriage to see if it'll work out."

Which of these statements doesn't fit? The last, obviously, but why? Are there solid, proven reasons not to cohabit? Yes.

It's clear that many people choose to live with a significant other without the added commitment of marriage.[7] It is sometimes seen as a kind of trial phase, a time to learn about each other and find out if you are compatible. Some of these couples may be monogamous and may be very much in love, but research indicates that this is a dangerous choice for their futures. Those who study this choice, also known as cohabitation, find that a large group of individuals enter that relationship with no plans at all of it ever becoming a marriage. They simply enjoy the comfort and convenience of living with and having sex with a person and are satisfied with that arrangement until something happens to make it unhappy and then they move on.

Cohabitation has become very common. In fact, by the age of twenty, approximately the same number of young people live in cohabiting relationships as are married (20 percent).[8] People entering a cohabiting relationship are often virgins before starting into this type of sexual relationship. All too often, cohabitation is a compromise—a partial commitment in exchange for the rights and benefits that research shows are enjoyed most in a lifelong commitment. Overwhelming evidence shows that an intimate relationship with an "out clause" generally does not fulfill the anticipation of those who choose such an arrangement. Rather than providing benefits, this type of relationship often produces problems.

Consider the following facts:

- Cohabiting relationships are not as permanent as marital relationships. The majority of cohabiting couples either break up or marry within two years.[9]
- Couples who live together and then get married face

a greater chance of divorcing than couples who never cohabited.[10]

- Cohabiting couples often get pregnant. Over a quarter of unmarried mothers are cohabiting at the time of their children's birth.[11]
- Lack of commitment is a standard attitude in cohabiting relationships. Even when cohabitors have been together for long periods of time, they often do not feel obligated to remain with this partner forever.[12]
- Cohabiting couples experience violent behavior much more often than married couples. Cohabiting couples are also much more likely than married couples to say that arguments between them have become physical.[13]

The reason for pointing out these characteristics of cohabitation is not to criticize people who have chosen this lifestyle (though these facts should forewarn individuals considering cohabitation or who are presently in such a relationship) but to indicate how the neurochemicals and the brain centers associated with love and sex seem to work and why the bonding that is so powerful in marriage seems less so in cohabiting relationships.

Research suggests that essentially every romantic physical contact between two people results in some degree of bonding.[14] However, such bonding requires reinforcement. We know from studies that cohabiting couples spend less time together than married couples do. This is due to a number of factors, including the fact that men who value personal leisure are more likely to enter a cohabiting relationship than to marry.[15] If couples are spending less time together they clearly have less time to hold hands, to hug, to touch, to stimulate the bonding chemicals in the brain to flow. For those chemicals to have the maximum effect they require almost daily activation by repeated closeness and touch. The finding that cohabiting couples often spend less time together may therefore explain why studies show that in general they enjoy sex less than married people.

Additionally, cohabitation is defined by a lack of commitment and a lack of sexual exclusivity.[16] These limitations are usually defined at the outset of the relationship and agreed to by both parties, thus limiting its potential to become truly intimate or last a lifetime. Cohabitors are also four times more likely than married individuals to report having been involved in infidelity; and behavior that can negatively affect the relationship by producing jealousy, guilt, dishonesty, and so on.[17] Lack of commitment to sexual fidelity is a standard attitude in cohabiting relationships. This lesser commitment to one's partner extends through all aspects of life, besides sexual fidelity. Cohabitors are less likely than spouses to view their sexual union as permanently exclusive. In a recent study, 16 percent of cohabiting men said they had been unfaithful during the past year alone.[18]

Studies clearly show that for both men and women, those who expected to be together a long time were more sexually satisfied with each other than those who had a short-term outlook.[19]

Another reason for cohabiting relationships to end sooner than marriages may be that individuals entering such a relationship generally knew their partner for a shorter period of time prior to moving in than their married peers.[20] This more abrupt consummation of a relationship can lead to errors in judgment about the other person. Also, remember that a woman can begin to trust a man because of oxytocin secretion and thus ignore the warning signs of an unwise relationship.

Ultimately, the happiness in a relationship is directly related to its expectation of long-term stability and exclusivity.[21] Cohabiting relationships, by definition, lack that key ingredient that helps seal neurochemical bonds and sustain two individuals for a lifetime.

We can now understand why cohabiting relationships are often less satisfying and happy than marriage relationships and why they break up more often. Even though the couple experiences bonding due to the presence of oxytocin and vasopressin, a long-term commitment is not a component of the relationship. The compromised nature of their relationship can actually overpower the neurochemical influence of those bonding mechanisms.

> "I was so naïve—he said we wouldn't go all the way but he kept pushing and we finally did it. Now I care about him but am angry at him all at the same time. I don't know if I can ever fully trust him again."
>
> —Gina, 18

Looking for love in all the wrong places

One of the most common relationships that lead a couple to engage in sex outside of marriage is the presence of some form of commitment, though limited. Sometimes these committed, nonmarital, monogamous relationships can last months or even years.

Yet without the true commitment that comes with marriage and the societal boundaries and support that come with it, long-term monogamy by itself often becomes a dead end. It is, statistically speaking, more likely to end early than a marriage is, less likely to be happy and fulfilling, and more likely to result in physical or psy-

> Being fully human means integrating our minds, spirits, and souls and working toward the goal of discovering our purpose for living on this planet.

chological abuse. It is not the ideal or the best and can be a counterfeit relationship that makes a couple feel that they are doing what is best when what they are actually doing is taking a significant risk.[22]

But the riskiest sexual situations by far are those that involve an increasing number of sexual partners with no commitment whatsoever. When individuals begin having sex with minimal or no commitment, it is often called "hooking up." This is a term so common now that it hardly needs explaining. Suffice it to say that surveys of college students indicate it can mean anything from kissing to oral sex to penetrative intercourse. A similar sexual relationship is often referred to as "friends with benefits," in which a couple decides to have sex whenever one or the other wants it but without any obligation, any promise or thought of a future relationship, and without any (intended) emotion for each other. Of course, many patterns of uncommitted sexual activity defy an easy label.[23] The one thing we know for sure is that such behavior is rampant among American young people. Though we touched on some of these in the previous chapter, it is worth reiterating and adding to these sobering facts. The following are some statistics to show how many teens and young adults are sexually involved:

High School Students
- Approximately 46 percent of all high school students (freshmen to seniors) have had sexual intercourse;[24]

- Over 50 percent of 15–19-year-olds have tried oral sex;[25]
- Approximately 11 percent of 15–19-year-olds have tried anal intercourse;[26]
- Approximately 75 percent of graduating high school seniors have had sexual intercourse;[27]
- Approximately 16 percent of high school students have had four or more sexual partners.[28]

College Students
- 70.2 percent of males and 70.9 percent of females have had sex with at least one partner in the past year;[29]
- 17 percent of males and 10.9 percent of females reported three or more sexual partners in the past year;[30]
- 45.2 percent of males and 45.1 percent of females reported having oral sex one or more times in the past 30 days.[31]

These alarming statistics corroborate much of what has already been mentioned. The younger teenagers are when they initiate sexual activity, the more sexual partners they will be likely to have had by the time they are interviewed again in their twenties. Sexual behavior for this young group, once it has commenced, appears almost compulsive. This certainty correlates with neuroscientific findings that sex has an addictive effect on the brain.

Numerous studies show that when people have had sex before marriage, they are more likely to divorce when they do marry later on.[32] Divorce, however, is not the sole measure of the health of one's attachment or connecting ability. Perhaps as important is the finding that individuals who have had sex before marriage are less likely to experience marital happiness. They are more likely to have difficulty adjusting to marriage and less likely to experience happiness, satisfaction, and love.[33]

This information indicates damage to the bonding process in the brain. Science clearly demonstrates that not everyone who has sex will experience these problems. However, some undoubtedly will. The problem is that a person cannot know if they will be one of those affected or not. It seems best therefore to not risk behavior that can have such significant negative impact on one's future.

Sex: any time, any place, any . . . body?

Consider these questions:

Why shouldn't we have sex whenever we want to with whomever we want to?

Since animals have, as do humans, all these brain hormones and sex hormones circulating, why don't animals experience love as humans do?

Why do dogs not feel emotional loss after they mate and then go their separate ways?

"After we began having sex I felt dead inside a lot. I almost felt like I was invisible, except when we would have sex. Then I would feel alive for those few minutes. I would crave sex for that feeling."

—Jennifer, 19

The major difference between humans and animals, from a purely physical perspective, is that human beings have the most highly developed prefrontal cortex of all creatures. We are not robots controlled by our brain hormones and sex hormones. Yes, the brain chemicals and their impact on our thoughts and desires are powerful. But we can control our actions. Indeed, to be fully human, we must. Therefore, in the early days of intense romance, we can forego sexual involvement and rationally think through the implications of the relationship with our prefrontal cortex. We can help our adolescents, college-age students, and unmarried young adults do this also. When individuals become involved in sex in ways that are casual, careless, or noncommitted, they are, consciously or unconsciously, attempting to separate sex from the rest of their personhood.

Human beings are more than physical beings with body parts that each do their thing. Human beings are not just mouths to eat with/lungs to breathe with/legs to walk with/eyes to see with/genital organs to have sex with.

No, we are beings that bring together in a whole package the function of our bodies, our minds, and our spirits. All this includes our personalities, our likes and dislikes, and our capacity to connect and integrate with others. This "wholeness" means that each of our body parts meld in such a way that when used they contribute to what we are as human beings.

But being fully human means more than that. It means integrating our minds, spirits, and souls into a unit working toward the goal of discovering our purpose for and living out that purpose on this planet.[34]

We have a responsibility to ourselves—to our health, our well-being, our future—and to the world, since each of us is part of a family, a community. Understanding this should encourage us, if we want to reach our fullest potential, to do things that are stretching, difficult, challenging, and may even seem unnatural to our natures. But it is only when we choose and learn to do those things that we grow into mature, responsible adults.

It may be that the biggest damage done by society's view of sex is the attempt to separate the sex act from the rest of what we are.[35] Not only has that hurt the enjoyment of sex itself, but it has hurt us as human beings. It has hurt us in one of the most fundamental aspects of our beings, our need for connectedness with another. Because sex is the most intimate connection we can have with another it requires the integration of *all we are* into that sexual involvement—our love, our commitment, our integrity, our bodies, our very lives—for all of our years. If sex is less than this, it is just an animal act, and in some ways we are performing like creatures because we are not practicing it as full human beings. Sex of this type can make a person "feel" close to their sexual partner when truly they are not close at all. Sex devoid of relationship focuses on the physical and can actually inhibit the best kind of growth in intimacy.[36]

> "After breaking up with the boy I lost my virginity to, it was never the same. I was always looking for that same feeling and I just couldn't find it. My relationships got shorter and shorter and I felt worse about myself every time they ended."
>
> —Ann, 31

Handle with care

It is probably evident by now that the research about the brain presented in this book points to why casual sex can have a negative emotional impact on an individual. The aftermath of these experiences goes far beyond feeling bad or being disappointed that a relationship didn't work out. Sexual bonding is a very intense experience—unconscious, yet very real. As new contributions from the field of neuroscience are made available, we know more about how the human brain and body are made to have meaningful connections even from before birth. When individuals have sexual relationships, they have involved more than a pleasant physical sensation and emotional response. Because of oxytocin in the woman's brain and vasopressin in the man's brain, connectedness and bonding do occur. Short-term sexual relationships may result in the brain's response with oxytocin and vasopressin, but they are more of a "quick fix" that do not qualify as the kind of long-term connecting the human needs for wholeness.

An individual who is sexually involved, then breaks up and then is sexually involved again, and who repeats this cycle again and again is in danger of negative emotional consequences. People who behave in this manner are acting against, almost fighting against, the way they are made to function. When connectedness and bonding form and then are quickly broken and replaced with another sexual relationship, it often actually causes damage to the brain's natural connecting or bonding mechanism.[37]

"What is love? I don't think I ever really knew, although I thought I did. Now I wonder if I have ever really loved or been loved. It all got so tangled with sex. I think it is going to take me a long time to get it all sorted out."

—Tim, 25

Such broken relationships repeated over and over are caused (at least in part) by the "addicting" nature of sex and also produce more of such "addiction." Individuals may become hooked on having sex, but they cannot immediately feel or know the results of this lifestyle and these sexual relations and how it is molding their brains.

Regrets

Other studies support the fact that young people involved in sex often experience a "wistfulness" or "question about what it would have been like" about their sexual involvement. In annual surveys conducted by the National Campaign to Prevent Teen Pregnancy (NCPT), significant majorities of high school students consistently report that they think all high school students should receive a strong abstinence message. Surprisingly, this view is supported by many students who have experienced sex, since we know that nearly three-fourths of them have been sexually active by graduation. This regret is further demonstrated by another finding of the NCPT: 70 percent of female high school students and 55 percent of male high school students who have had sex reported that they wish they had waited.[38]

These short-term, damaging, and often regretted relationships undermine the purpose of bonding hormones such as oxytocin and vasopressin and the purpose of the brain compounding the excitement of sex by producing dopamine. These processes are present to contribute to what life is all about, to the purpose of our being including family and community and personal goals and happiness. Sex outside of the appropriate circumstances distorts the reason we have those brain responses and often negatively alters the courses of our lives.

> "I see what sex has done to some of my friends and their relationships. I know although I am tempted now, that my choice to say no will protect my heart and my body for the future. I try to remember that as I try to make good choices."
>
> —Laura, 16

But not the end of the story

Many people by now realize they—or their children or their friends—have been caught in the cycle of broken relationships or compulsion to continue sexual relationships that are harmful or even destructive. They may know the residue of problems from past behaviors and be discouraged. However, the human spirit is strong, and no one should feel he or she cannot change or find a way out of the cycle. There are ways. It may be a spiritual rebirth. It may be a firm decision and a strong will. It may be counseling. It may be committing to a group that agrees to help each other be accountable in their battle with sexual addiction or other behaviors.

While the brain of the fully developed adult is not as pliable as it is during the adolescent years, it is still moldable until death. Molding based on experience can continue to take place. Spiritual change, counseling, supportive peers, and group meetings that include encouragement for change are all experiences that can remold the brain.

A decision to make a change in behavior patterns is hard and takes courage, but it is necessary for many people to do if they want to be the most completely fulfilled person they can be—and to accomplish the goals they desire and are capable of.

Psychiatrist Norman Doidge, M.D., states, "The brain can change itself. It is a plastic, living organ that can actually change its own structure and function, even into old age."[39] Peter Eriksson of Sweden's Sahlgrenska University Hospital discovered that brains well into their sixties and seventies undergo "neurogenesis," [40] or the development of new brain cells. This is very encouraging information for individuals who are experiencing problems they desire to overcome—some of which may be traced to the way they were parented, some from abuse, but often from behavior choices they themselves made.

Some would say that problems individuals might encounter from past sexual activity with multiple partners or that started at a young age is natural and simply a part of life. Guys want to have sex. Girls want to have sex (and often agree to sex to have "love"). So people have sex whenever they feel they are ready because it seems that is the way they are made. However, just because a thought or behavior is natural does not necessarily make it appropriate or good.

> The human spirit is strong, and no one should feel he or she cannot change or find a way out of the cycle of broken relationships.

The late M. Scott Peck, M.D., in his book *The Road Less Traveled*, made some revealing statements about "just doing what is natural." He says, "The tendency to avoid challenge is so omnipresent in human beings that it can properly be considered a characteristic of human nature. But calling it natural does not mean it is essential or beneficial or unchangeable behavior. It is also natural to defecate in our pants and never brush our teeth. Yet we teach ourselves to do the unnatural until the unnatural becomes itself second nature."[41]

We remember things that did not come naturally to us, yet by working on that behavior we could accomplish it in such a way that it contributed to our life and our goals. So it is with sexual behavior.

Ultimately, it is easier and better for the adolescent and young adult brain to be molded and hardwired to habitually avoid destructive and life-limiting behaviors in the first place. This helps avoid as much as possible the necessity of engaging in the difficult job of remolding as an adult. It also clears the way for a happy and healthy future, free of the emotional and psychological baggage that comes with a past filled with sexual mistakes.

to THINK ABOUT

♦ Why isn't cohabitation as good an idea as it seems on the surface? Consider not only social implications, but what we know about the brain.

♦ Why can casual sex have a negative emotional impact on a person?

♦ How can we train ourselves to do what is difficult or what does not come naturally?

YOUNG PEOPLE ARE FULL OF HOPE.
They want to be accepted and truly valued for who they are. They need authentic relationships that are stable and loving in character.

Chapter Six

THE PURSUIT OF HAPPINESS

> "The hardest breakup I ever had was with the first person I had sex with. Fifteen years later, I still don't think I'm over him. I still dream about him and think about him and compare every guy since then to him. I'm married now and I feel like it's a threesome in my heart. He is still here. It is like he is a part of me and I still can't get over him."
>
> —Jordi, 33

We have revealed scientific data throughout this book that proves there are physical changes in the brain that occur as a result of past experience. We have emphasized that the behavior and experience of today can cause our brains to gel in such a way that good *or* bad habits develop and that our brains "make" us continue either good or bad behavior as a matter of course because that is "who we have become."

But we human beings and our behavior are much more complex than that, and parents, guardians, mentors, teachers, and anyone else involved in the life of a young person can be a powerful influence for good.[1] How do we get this information into the hands and heads of young people?

In survey after survey, in countless scientific studies

and polls, young people consistently say that the individuals in their lives who influence their behavior choices the most are their parents. Even college students report similar levels of trust toward their parents. Unfortunately, the only people who seem to be unaware of this fact are the parents themselves.[2]

This truth offers a golden opportunity for parents—and mentors and others who have the trust and confidence of young people—to guide them to constructive behavioral choices and away from destructive choices. A recent study by C. McNeely and coauthors showed that an overwhelming majority of teens who talked to their parents about sex rely on their parents rather than peers for information about sex.[3]

Parents have a number of advantages over other adult role models (teachers, health care professionals, clergy/youth ministers, coaches) when communicating with teenagers. Parents can discuss topics that are consistent with their values and select the most appropriate time and the most appropriate manner for the discussion. Parents have an intuitive sense of their adolescent's particular personality and sensitivities, external circumstances, maturity level, as well as social, emotional, physical, and moral development. In addition, parents are going to be with their young people year after year, providing continuing guidance and positive influence.[4]

Finally, parents know that sex cannot be separated from a larger, whole person interaction between two people. Sex is an intimate part of the love and relationship between two people. Sex is a part of the "stuff of life" including marriage, home, commitment, children, family, and all the rest. Parents also know that the physical sexual relationship matures, grows in depth of meaning between the husband and wife, grows in intimacy including the physical exploration of each other's bodies because such growing physical intimacy requires a level of trust that takes years to flourish and blossom.[5]

Parents know that none of this is possible with short-term sexual experiences through hooking up or "friends with benefits" or even relationships of several months that are sexual in nature. Parents know that young people who are engaged in short-term sexual relationships are cheating themselves out of authentic, fulfilling, and meaningful sex.[6]

> "What if they find out their Dad and I had sex before we got married? And here we are telling them not to. They'll see that we turned out okay and draw their own conclusions."
>
> —Erin, 33

What they don't know can hurt them

A key to understanding the importance of providing guidance to young people is recognizing that the adolescent brain still has a lot of developing to do. We have learned that until an individual reaches his mid-twenties, he is not fully equipped to make the most mature behavioral decisions.[7] This does *not* mean teenagers are inherently incapable of making decisions or unworthy of trust and respect. Many young people make excellent decisions throughout their teen years and demonstrate impressive levels of maturity. Sometimes this is the result of parents who provide healthy guidance. Occasionally it is through the experience of seeing parents make such bad mistakes that the young person becomes determined to do things differently.[8] But the vast majority of adolescents are not as well equipped, scientifically speaking, to make difficult judgments as they will be after their brains have fully developed.

If parents are unable or unwilling to provide guidance and counsel to their children, they are leaving their young people to make decisions they do not have the physical brain development to make. Such parents are abandoning their children at the time they need mature guidance the most. The result is often risky behavior practiced with sex, drugs, violence, and so on, many times with disastrous results.[9]

> "I don't want my kids to do what I did. I had no idea how my sexual past would affect the rest of my life. I worry my kids won't listen to my advice since they know I made very different choices, and in their eyes I seem fine."
>
> —Tory, 36

Is that a fact?

With the scientific information we provided in this book, parents can confidently talk to their children with facts. Many parents have advised their children to remain virgins until marriage because it was the moral choice they wanted their children to follow and was the value they had established in their own home. These are vital factors that every parent needs to make clear to their own children. Far too many teenagers admit confusion or ignorance when asked what their family's values are regarding sex.[10] It is comforting and encouraging for parents to know that in addition to their own morals and values, they can now offer scientific support for their guidance.

Parents can now confidently say that science shows that for young people to have the best chance of a happy life, they should wait until they are in a lifelong committed relationship before having sex. This information can make it easier to enter into a conversation that is hard for almost all parents to initiate. This information can make the parent more confident in the conversation. They can know that they are presenting facts, and not just giving their opinion that refraining from sex before marriage—and anticipating it within marriage—is the best choice.

> "Talking to my girls about sex is just so awkward. I don't feel like I know what to say—what is enough and what is too much. What if they ask me questions about my past? Then what do I say?"
>
> —Robert, 39

They are paying attention—now what?

Parents who are confronted with the information about sexually transmitted infections, nonmarital pregnancy, and the emotional risks associated with adolescent and young adult sexual involvement often ask what they can do to help their children avoid such problems. Here again research helps provide direction.

The first thing parents should realize is that even if they have had a conversation about sexual issues with their child, the child can often remain confused about their parents' expectations for them.[11] Research indicates that parents and mentors need to reinforce over and over the messages they want young people to understand. Otherwise, teenagers will remain confused about what is expected of them concerning sexual and other behavior. In today's environment, if they do not have clear messages from their parents about family values they are more susceptible to sexual invitations from friends when offered.

When conversations do occur, parents often do not communicate about sexual matters clearly enough for their children to understand. A recent study of African American adolescents aged fourteen to seventeen years revealed conflicting recollections about such conversations with their mothers. The percentage of mothers (73 percent) who strongly agreed with the statement "I have talked with my teen about sex" differed from the percentage of teens (46 percent) who strongly agreed with the statement "my mother has talked to me about sex."[12] This shows, if nothing else, that one conversation about sex and sexual behavior is not enough. No longer is it considered adequate to have "The Talk" at a certain age. It needs to be an ongoing conversation, year after year. Daily experiences, questions about school or work, or any opportunity can be taken advantage of to make conversation while riding in the car or sitting at the dinner table.

After all, studies clearly show that parental involvement has a definite impact on a young person's behavior choices.[13] For instance,

- teens whose parents express disapproval of non-marital sex and contraceptive use are less likely than their peers to have sex.[14]
- adolescents who perceive parental disapproval of sexual activity are less likely to become sexually active.[15]
- teens who talk to a parent about initiating sex tend to wait and ultimately have fewer sexual partners.[16]

Unfortunately, studies also show that many parents do not talk to their teens about sex.[17] Perhaps the data that has been presented about the influence parents have on their children will help a parent keep on talking, even when their child is resistant or appears uninterested, when in reality they are all the time listening and being guided by the parent more than any other influence.

In addition, it is absolutely critical for parents to be good role models. If, for example, a parent smokes, it is difficult for them to honestly tell their child that it is unhealthy to smoke and expect their child to not smoke. Similarly, if the home is a single-parent home and that parent is having friends in for sex, it is less likely that telling a young person to avoid sex until marriage is going to be highly effective. It still is the best message but may have less effect.[18]

"But when I was young I . . . "

> "I'm afraid my kids will find out about some of the things I did. They'll see that I turned out okay and think that they will too."
>
> —Carolyn, 40

Many parents who grew up in the sixties, seventies, and eighties were sexually active in their youth and did not experience sexually transmitted infections or nonmarital pregnancies. This group often struggles with feeling hypocritical when advising their children to not be involved sexually. They need to understand that the adolescent sexual environment has changed markedly since they were young. For example, in the 1960s there were only two sexually transmitted infections of much concern: gonorrhea and syphilis. Both were treatable at the time with penicillin. Today, there are more than twenty-five sexually transmitted infections worthy of serious concern. Most of these diseases are viral and, though there are drugs to suppress some of them, none of the viral diseases can be cured.[19] Only one in fifty adolescents in the 1960s was infected with a sexually transmitted disease. Today, one of four sexually active adolescents is infected.[20]

As we have seen, the factor that is missing from both

statistics are the unexpected psychological risks young people are taking when they are sexually involved. Such information has not been available in the past. Because of all these things it is not hypocritical, but indeed is the only appropriate thing for parents who were sexually active in their past to do—encourage their children to seek one person to be with for their whole lives, and to share themselves with only that person.

> "No one was interested in me before. I don't think I am as cute as some of my friends and I don't hang out with popular kids. I have to go all the way with boys for them to like me. I'd rather have sex than be alone again."
>
> —Rachel, 16

It took a village

Young people will not have all the guidance and support they need if it is only their parents who are providing such guidance. While parents are the first and most important voices for young people, teenagers and young adults benefit the most when not only their parents but all of society around them is giving them guidance toward the most healthy choices.[21]

One of the most effective programs for reducing teen sexual activity and teen pregnancy focused on just such a community-oriented approach. Carried out in the rural town of Denmark, South Carolina, the program enlisted all the influential groups of the town to advise and guide their young people to avoid sexual activity. The program involved the schools, churches, business organizations, physicians, newspapers, and parents giving the same message. The results were phenomenal. Local pregnancy rates declined by more than 50 percent from 1981 to 1985. In contrast, the pregnancy rates for the surrounding communities rose by almost 20 percent over the same time period. By 1988, just three years after the program was discontinued, the pregnancy rate had bounced back up and even exceeded pre-program levels.[22]

Although there has been some controversy about exactly how the program worked in this town, there is no controversy that the entire community joined together to give their young people one message—sexual activity and the resulting pregnancies were not good for them and for their future. No one disputes the amazing outcome that was of enormous benefit to hundreds of young people through a community that united in helping their children have a better future.

A Change in Behavior

We know that many young adults—and older ones too—have made mistakes in the past. So what happens next? Is it too late? Has the brain been so molded that there is no hope for a happy, productive future? For many readers, this is a difficult question. No one can change what has happened in the past—what's done is done, and we can't rewrite history, no matter how much some of us would like to. Instead, each person must look to the future and decide how the rest of their story will unfold.

For some, the next chapter in their life story may mean reclaiming their virginity, sometimes called "secondary virginity," by changing behavior and setting new standards in their relationships.[23] For others, the next step to a great future may mean avoiding difficult situations and creating new dating rules to maintain their virginity.[24] Some are left with the painful psychological scars of sexual abuse or manipulation that they must work through to become whole again.[25] Each path presents challenges that can be difficult to overcome. Young people might wonder, with some justification: *What if my boyfriend or girlfriend can't accept changes in our relationship and chooses to leave? What if my friends see me differently because of this change in my life? Does this mean I will be left out of the fun and excitement of high school or college because I'm not doing what everyone else seems to be doing?*[26]

And the scariest: *What if the sadness and shame of a past mistake never stops?*

More than just saying no

> "All my friends at school are having sex . . . or at least saying they are. Virgins get made fun of. People think you are super-religious or weird or something. And everyone gossips about what everyone else is doing."
>
> —Derek, 17

For most readers, whether they have had sex before or not, the conclusion is obvious: the healthiest choice is to wait and experience sex in a lifelong, faithful, committed relationship, rarely accomplished except in marriage.[27] For many, that will mean a drastic change in behavior. For others, it means sustaining and remaining committed to a choice that has already been made. In either case, it's not always easy. As young people grow and mature, they are better able to guide their own behavior and make the right choices. For teenagers and young adults up to their mid-twenties, that process can be more difficult. That's why it is critical for parents, guardians, mentors, teachers, and other adults to understand the culture, know the facts, and offer the healthiest and most effective help and support.

Research has confirmed what common sense would tell us. In a report published in the *Journal of the American Med-*

ical Association,[28] Michael D. Resnick, Ph.D., and his coauthors showed that adolescents who were strong enough to avoid sexual involvement had three primary things in common:

- high levels of parent-family connectedness,
- parental disapproval of the adolescent becoming sexually active, and
- parental disapproval of the adolescent using contraception.

The study clearly defined the involvement of parents with their children in which there was "high levels of parent-family connectedness." These characteristics included "feelings of warmth, love, and caring from parents" as well as "physical presence of a parent in the home at key times." Key times were clearly defined as a parent being present before school, after school, at dinner, and bedtime. Most adolescents, even through college age, say that the most influential people regarding their behavior choices are their parents.[29] That being said, here are some practical suggestions to offer young people that can help them avoid sexual entanglements, thus preserving their best chance of a bright future.

⮕ Find a good friend with the same commitment about sex.

This is someone to share values, secrets, plans, and dreams with. Talk about fears and temptations, and lean on each other for strength. Many people find tremendous strength simply by being able to share their feelings with someone who understands and relates to them.[30]

➡ *Write down your commitment to abstain from sex.*

Collect motivational quotes or other thoughts, write them on index cards, and keep them as a reminder. Take them out to read during stressful times, add to your collection as you learn and grow, and share them with someone you trust.[31]

➡ *Practice assertiveness.*

It can be difficult to stand your ground when friends, dates, or significant others pressure you into doing something you know is unhealthy and unsafe. Every person has the right to make decisions concerning their own body, especially when your health, future, and well-being is at stake. Take time to talk about your rights and how you expect to be treated. Practice discussing your reasons for abstaining with parents or a friend.[32]

➡ *Make sure your values are known to anyone you date or grow close with.*

It is critical for someone who is attracted to you to understand the boundaries and limitations of the relationship. Making your views clear early on can lay the foundation for a rewarding relationship—or help you steer clear of one that was doomed to fail.[33]

➡ *Don't get involved with someone who doesn't share your values.*

Talk about your plans for the future and be clear about your expectations. If you are interested in someone who can't support your decisions and accept you for who you are, put a stop to the relationship and wait for someone who will.[34]

Plan your dates to avoid difficult situations.

Don't just get together in private places and see what happens. Find fun things to do with others or in public and keep the focus of the relationship where it should be.[35]

Avoid alcohol and drugs. Aside from all the other obvious risks,

they will impair judgment and make tough decisions more difficult. Remember, it isn't always about your own judgment—your date won't be thinking clearly either. This is a serious concern in situations where a male is much bigger and stronger than a female, or in a place where there is no help nearby.[36]

Introduce your date to your parents.

Your parents will appreciate it, and it will communicate a great deal about what you value and how you expect to be treated. Parents can offer better support and guidance when they know the people involved.[37] Parents can be more objective about a potential date than young people, as they are not susceptible to the trust and bonding processes already discussed in this book.

Limit the amount of physical contact.

Set boundaries with your boyfriend or girlfriend early on in the relationship and stick to them. Conflict often arises because of unrealistic expectations or surprises. Communicating the rules beforehand eliminates that threat and lays the foundation for a healthy relationship.[38]

> "Sex doesn't make a relationship. You don't have to have sex to be in a relationship."
>
> —Tamika, 20

Just say yes

Human behavior is complicated, and our scientific understanding of it is still very incomplete. In reality, what can happen is that the well-developed human prefrontal cortex, the center of human decision making, can trump the neurochemical functions we have discussed in this book. Though the influence of neurochemicals is strong, we are not slaves to it.

No matter what a person's genetic predisposition or background is, he or she can still make good decisions about behavior with their prefrontal cortex, decisions to avoid risky behavior. This is not a surprise but instead affirms what we have said throughout this book and will continue to say until the end. We don't know everything about the brain, but we do know some things, and these things can help give guidance to the behavior choices that can contribute the most to our personal and long-term fulfillment and to the best future for our children.

Young people are full of hope. They want to be accepted and truly valued for who they are. They need this in the context of authentic relationships with parents and other adults. These authentic relationships must be stable and loving in character. They intuitively know that "boundaries" mandated by those who love them are actually a sign of being loved and valued. Teenagers may rail and fight against boundaries at times, but if they know they are provided with loving care by parents with whom they have a good relationship, they will usually not go behind parents' backs and cross those boundaries. [39]

Teens fear being alone and not belonging. They fear that they may not actually measure up and that this fact will be found out even though they may be a leader and perform well in athletics, academics, or whatever endeavor they are engaged in. They want relationships with adults and they want to be taken seriously by them.[40]

Compelling activities must be provided for young people or, because of the way their brains are made, they will often find excitement on their own. Their brains demand the excitement of dopamine input. The diversions we provide them must be within parameters that keep them from experiencing activities that could be dangerously molding their brains to produce unhealthy behavior choices in the future, besides being dangerous to their physical health. Providing young people with interesting things to do

There are many healthy activities that young people can take part in that can protect their present health and contribute to their future.

and encouraging them to do exciting things must be understood in light of this new information, that the experiences they are having are literally molding their brains in ways that can be either beneficial or detrimental.[41]

There are so many exciting activities that young people can take part in that can protect their present health and contribute to their future that it would be impossible to list them all. But the suggestions listed here can offer the dopamine high that young people are born to seek out, and help them get hooked on pursuits other than sexual activity.

Academics. Almost all young people can benefit from achievement in the scholastic arena of their lives. Many of the rewards are obvious: more college and other higher educational opportunities, better jobs, and so on, as well as the pleasure of learning new things and being exposed to an abundance of information. However, parents need to realize there are great emotional rewards from achievement itself. Young people desperately want to feel like they belong, connect, and fit in with the world around them. Succeeding in the classroom can be a critical part of that process and can also give them feelings of great excitement and satisfaction.

Fine arts. Young people can find real fulfillment in expressing themselves in music, drama, painting, sculpting, or any number of other creative pursuits. The commitment to practice an instrument, for example, over the long-term is good evidence of a healthy addiction to the dopamine reward.

Athletics. Sports for both males and females are a wonderful area of achievement and dopamine reward for young people. In addition, athletics are healthy for the physical development of young bodies and can teach teamwork, problem solving, and also provide a positive environment to meet friends.

Volunteer and philanthropic work. Meaningful work includes tasks and challenges that contribute to the home, neighborhood, and community. In addition to the reward of completing a project, young people can learn that persistence pays off and that such an experience is very fulfilling. An additional reward is that young people can learn everyday skills by doing such tasks, skills that they may be able to use as adults.

Further, whether helping the homeless, visiting a nursing home, helping a disabled person who lives next door, or going on a missions trip with a youth group, there are plenty of opportunities for young people to be involved in doing good. Such activities can offer complex challenges and rich emotional rewards.

Spiritual development. Many young people find that practicing their faith is an exceedingly rewarding part of their life and that holding faith is directly related to other positive outcomes in their lives. Faith can challenge their minds, encourage discipline and hard work, and connect them with others in a positive context.

Letting Go

As we have seen, dopamine serves a vital function in the lives of young people. It makes them look forward to independence, to living as adults separate from their parents, and starting the cycle of life again: marrying, having children, raising those children, and then one day seeing them leave as well. Because of the dopamine effect, young people are excited about the thrill of their future, even though it is scary, uncertain, and not yet mapped out. Good parents realize that this is why they have been giving their children guidance, so they can become successful adults themselves. Without the stimulating influence of dopamine, young people might begin evaluating the pros and cons of moving out and decide that the safest thing to do is to just stay home with their parents. After all, their parents have a house, a job with regular income, and have already figured out how the world works. So why leave? However, because of the dopamine reward for doing exciting things, there is a restlessness that cannot be satisfied by staying safe and secure at home with parents.

> "I never realized how nervous I would be about Angela's college years until we waved good-bye to her. Then I worried for weeks about whether or not I had taught her the right things, warned her about boys, and helped her to be ready."
>
> —Eddie, 37

Individuals vary in their readiness for this stage of life. Some are terrified and some can't wait for complete independence. However, almost all in some sense experience an excitement about the events of this time of life as a result of the dopamine high.

This can be a scary time for parents, because whether they know it consciously or just sense it intuitively, they know that some young people get hurt in the process of becoming independent. However, it is still vital for parents to gradually but finally let go.[42]

A whole person

> "After I accepted the challenge to model the abstinent behavior for my teenage daughter, I expected to feel different. But I had no idea I would feel so clean."
>
> —Jennifer, 37

No matter how supportive an environment is provided for a child there is no guarantee that that individual child will always make good behavior decisions. Some children, raised in the very best homes with two loving parents to raise them, will still make poor choices of behavior and experience problems as a result. Some of the problems they encounter can limit their opportunities, can affect them for the rest of their lives, and can keep them from ever accomplishing the things they had always dreamed of.

Conversely, no matter how bad the environment a child is raised in some will overcome the disadvantage of their origins and excel. Some children seem to be formed from before birth to make good choices, to not be as influenced by their peers, by media, or by other negative influences as other young people are. Some seem born with or seem to develop a spiritual sensitivity that serves as a guiding light to their behavior.[43]

No matter how accurate or revealing our new neuroscience is about how the brain functions, it does not "tell all" about the totality of human behavior. Human behavior is much more complicated than that. The truth is that we are just beginning to scratch the surface of knowledge about human sexual behavior.[44] However, just be-

> *Science shows that those who abstain from sex until marriage significantly add to their chance for avoiding problems and finding happiness.*

cause our knowledge is not complete does not mean that we do not know some things. We dare not ignore what we do know just because we don't know everything!

We know that humans are not just a mass of muscle, fat, organs, and water. We will never be fully explained by scientific or chemical analysis. We want to emphasize that we do not mean to imply that people who are sexually abstinent until marriage have discovered the secret to all of life. We do not mean to imply that if people have had sex before or outside marriage they have totally destroyed their potential. However, the most current research shows that people who have been involved in premarital and/or extramarital sex have significantly added to their chance of having problems and significantly increase their risk of never achieving their potential for health, hope, and happiness; and that those who abstain from sex until marriage significantly add to their chance for avoiding problems and finding happiness.

to THINK ABOUT

◆ What do parents have to offer their teens and young adult children?

◆ Is it possible to overcome past mistakes? How?

◆ The authors claim that "young people are filled with hope." Should they be? Why? What healthy goals, pursuits, dreams can adults guide them to?

THERE IS MUCH MORE TO THE HUMAN
experience than we could ever explain.

Chapter Seven

FINAL THOUGHTS

> "It wasn't easy, but I am so glad we waited. I'm healthy, I love my wife, and I just don't have the baggage some of my friends do."
>
> —Rick, 30

A quick glance in any bookstore, newsstand, on the Internet, or at television programs will confirm that Americans have a new fascination with the brain. Books and articles abound with stories on Alzheimer's, IQ tests, headaches, and any other topic that relates to the all-important three-pound mass that sits between our ears.

This fascination with the wellspring of our thoughts and awareness that has exploded in recent years is due in large part to fundamental discoveries in our knowledge of the brain. Recent and increasingly sophisticated studies of the brain have presented startling discoveries to researchers on questions that have baffled science for generations. These advances have allowed us to understand so much more about why we do what we do.

The reason a book like this one is even possible is that new neuroscience techniques for studying the brain have proliferated over the past fifteen years. Relying on MRI technology and other scanning and imaging techniques, we

simply know more about the brain now than we did twenty
or thirty years ago.

Of course, we aren't even close to knowing everything
about the brain. In fact, the more we discover, the more we
understand how complex the brain really is.[1] Countless
questions remain unanswered. But we do know enough to
inform people in practical ways about a great deal that is
happening in their heads and what to do with this new information.

In previous chapters we have discussed much of this
abundant new data about the brain. Our focus has been on
the information that applies to connectedness, attachment,
addiction, infatuation, love, sex, monogamy, marriage, and
other issues related to our sexual behavior and our sexual
health. The data indicates that sexuality and sexual behavior are a vital part of what makes us human—it is scientifically and behaviorally inaccurate to try to understand sexual
activity as though it has no impact on the rest of what we are
as human beings: our emotions, our health, our habits, and
our nature. Sex is far too integral to who and what we are as
persons to do this. We cannot separate the brain from the
body. What our bodies do has a dramatic impact on our
brains (and all that happens there, including emotions, and so on),
and what we think in our brains will have a dramatic impact on
our bodies and how we use them.[2]

> "My parents tell me not to
> have sex, but they never
> explain why. They just say
> that it's wrong and sinful.
> I'm sick of hearing the same
> thing over and over."
>
> —Kelly, 17

The doctor says . . .

Many decisions about sexual
behavior directly affect an individual's physical and emotional
health both now and in the fu-

ture. Because of that reality, this book is designed to function as a caring and good doctor would—one who is concerned about preventive medicine and wants patients to avoid problems so they can have the best chance for a healthier future with as few problems as possible. Such a doctor, though capable of helping a person overcome a health problem through medicine or surgery, is even more interested in helping the person avoid the problem in the first place.

For example, a doctor may see a patient who is drinking excessively. The doctor would likely tell the patient that while alcoholic beverages are not intrinsically harmful (except during pregnancy), excessive use can damage the body. In addition, the person who drinks excessively has a negative impact not only on himself but on those around him at work and at home. A good doctor then recommends appropriate and healthy use of alcohol according to the science about such behavior while giving the warnings about what can happen if such advice is not followed. This advice is not a moral judgment and is not a statement on the value of the person or their life choices. If the patient returns having made no behavior change, the physician does not consider it a moral failing and is not critical. The doctor merely reiterates the pattern for a healthy lifestyle and encourages it again without giving up on the patient or compromising what science says is the healthiest behavior choice.

In the same way, in this book we have made recommendations for the sexual behavior choices that offer the greatest chance to avoid what could be life-changing problems. Some of these recommendations may be unpopular. Some are unexpected and run counter to popular culture. Abstinence culminating in a lifelong committed relationship (it is rare for couples involved in a sexual relationship to maintain that relationship for life unless it is in the context of their being married[3]) has long been perceived as a religious position rather than a suggested course of action based on scientific reality.

But now, with the aid of modern neuroscience and a wealth of research, it is evident that humans are the healthiest and happiest when they engage in sex only with the one who is their mate for a lifetime.[4]

In the past, medical recommendations for sexual behavior were based on science that did not have the benefit of today's research and technology. MRI and other sophisticated brain imaging tools were simply not available until recent years. Consequently, societal recommendations about this important area of life were formed that did not account for the powerful and verifiable connection between sex and brain function; and they were based more on personal philosophy, prejudice, and ideology than any verifiable science.

Unfortunately, poor recommendations based on these shaky foundations still persist.

However, modern breakthroughs in neuroscience research techniques and this new data now accumulating are leading to a major change in approach to sexual behavior understanding and recommendations.[5] The science says that generally speaking, the healthiest behavior, both physically and emotionally, is for persons to abstain from sex until they can commit to one partner for the rest of their life.[6] Some will follow that recommendation. Others will not. However, we can now safely say that it is a suggested course of action based on scientific reality.

More than that, as we consider all the data we have reviewed in this book, we are drawn to the conclusion that modern evolutionary theory about human sexuality is wrong. This theory can be summarized by saying that those who propose it believe that human beings are (their terms) "designed" to be promiscuous. The fundamental theory is that women have sex with various men until they find the one with the best genes. Men have sex with various women until one chooses him to father her child. [7]

What we have shown in the data we have discussed is just the opposite of this theory. It appears that the most up-to-date research suggests that most humans are "designed' to be sexually monogamous with one mate for life. This information also shows that the further individuals deviate from this behavior, the more problems they encounter, be they STDs, nonmarital pregnancy, or emotional problems, including damaged ability to develop healthy connectedness with others, including future spouses.

And finally, as we have discussed, most young people think it is best that they be guided to abstinence (90 percent); most of them plan to be married (90 percent), and indeed by age thirty, that percentage are married.

Now what?

The science presented in this book and the conclusions drawn from it will have different effects on different people. Those who are single and abstinent will probably feel affirmed by what they have learned. Individuals who have been faithfully married for many years will perhaps be encouraged

> "The hardest thing about encouraging my kids to be abstinent is looking in the mirror and knowing that I wasn't. They wonder why it is such a big deal to me. If they ever found out everything I have been through, they would understand."
>
> —Richard, 41

and understand more about their ability to stay together through all the trials of a lifelong partnership. Individuals who are living with a boyfriend or girlfriend, those who change sexual partners occasionally, and those who, though not living together, are in love and having sex may be made uncomfortable by what they have heard.

Before dismissing what modern scientific research tells us about ourselves because of where we are in life or because of our sexual decisions of the past, let this information enlighten you. For example, if you are in a sexual relationship that just seems "right" but your partner leaves or cheats on you and you feel used and misled, consider those feelings in light of what you now know about the bonding impact of sexual involvement. If you are married or cohabiting and have had multiple sexual partners in the past, accept the fact that the research revealed in this book shows that your bonding mechanism may be compromised and you have a greater risk of failing to maintain a commitment to the marriage. Therefore, if cracks start showing up in the relationship, do something about it right away without hesitation. That "something" may be marriage counseling, attending a marriage seminar, or sometimes just talking to a trusted friend. Those who have been sexually abused in some way can use this information as validating their inner feelings that something is not right and motivate them to seek counseling. These are but a few examples of how this information can benefit your life.

The tip of the iceberg

Another critical finding of the neuroscience research is that sex cannot be dismissed as an activity with little or no impact on the person as a whole. We know sex involves the entire individual, the whole person. Perhaps the most

> "When we broke up I just ached all over. I didn't miss having sex, but I missed having him so much more than I ever thought I would. I still don't understand what happened to me."
>
> —Cheryl, 19

damaging philosophy about sex in recent years has been the attempt to separate sex from the whole person. Neuroscientific evidence has revealed this approach to be not only false but also dangerous.[8] Popular culture would have you believe that young people should become involved in sex when they feel "ready" and that to not become involved sexually at that point in their lives will cause them to be sexually naive and repressed.[9] As we've seen, the facts tell a very different story.

The new neuroscience research shows us that the human mind is an astounding organ and one we will never totally comprehend. But beyond that, just as the brain is infinitely complex, it is even more difficult to fully grasp what it means to be fully human. There is much more to the human experience than we can ever explain. Life is not just a collection of choices, nor are we robots or mechanical beings who hopelessly get hooked on certain behavior. And to think that we are nothing more than a group of "brain cells" or neurochemicals moved about by our environment is ridiculous. We cannot be explained by quantity, matter, or motion. However, we do know and understand some things about ourselves. This information, properly interpreted and utilized, gives us direction toward the most beneficial behavior choices. This allows us so much new insight into how to live in harmony with our innate nature and therefore to be more fully human. The neuroscience we have explored in this book shows us that the human brain is not just a cold mechanical computer, processing information, but a living organ shaped by love and emotion and kindness as well as by trauma and hurt and insult, among other things.

The findings we present in this book are but the tip of the iceberg of what will be discovered about the brain in the next fifty years. But as we have said, just because we don't know everything does not mean that what we do know is of no consequence. The findings we report here are verifiable. The lessons drawn from the facts we present here are practical because they reflect the way humans are wired. The behavior recommendations are realistic and reasonable because they are based on reliable information of who we are and how we function best because of our human nature.

We look forward to more study of the human brain. Not only will future findings be exciting and interesting, but they will help us understand more of how we function best because of how we are made.

ACKNOWLEDGMENTS

This book is the result of years of ongoing study of the emerging research regarding human sexual behavior by The Medical Institute for Sexual Health. Throughout its existence, the men and women of this organization have been dedicated to this work. *Hooked* would not have been written without the foundation of credible research, study, and data evaluation and collection produced by The Medical Institute.

Lynne Lutz, Psy.D., a practicing clinical psychologist in Dallas, Texas, working primarily with women, has provided the powerful quotes found throughout the text. William Ruwe, Ph.D., a neuropsychologist working with the NeuroResources organization in Oklahoma City, Oklahoma, has provided invaluable resources and vital validation for the research on which this book is founded. David Hager, M.D., gave us encouragement to embark on this book when it was only a fledgling idea, a great help.

Finally, Jon Yarian, working with the Pinkston Group of Alexandria, Virginia, has taken our scientific scribbling and turned it into text that is organized, readable, and understandable. Without Jon the valuable information we are providing here would have been much more poorly organized and much more difficult to understand and therefore much less useful.

The cutting-edge information contained in this book comes from the evolutionary process of the work of the many competent physicians and scientists affiliated with The Medical Institute. It is impossible to name all of the wonderfully dedicated people who work or have worked there. However, acknowledgment of certain specific individuals who have laid the foundation for this book is a must. First among those to be thanked are the president and CEO, Gary Rose, M.D. Without his unflagging enthusiasm and support this book would not have happened.

Dr. Rose's executive assistant, Kim French, has coordinated so many details of this project that it would make a normal person dizzy. Kate Hendricks, M.D., M.P.H., T.M., director of the Science Department of the Medical Institute and her staff, both present and past, have studied huge quantities of newly emerging data that are opening up understanding of human sexual behavior in a way never possible in the past because of lack of modern research and human evaluation techniques.

The Medical Institute librarian, Harold Thiele, provided valuable service retrieving references for this work. Others at the Medical Institute who have contributed are: Patricia Thickstun, Leslie Romoli, Amy Campbell, Art Coleman, Jean Marie McLain, Alejandra Eckel, and Gladys Gonzales. Four past members of The Medical Institute Science Department deserve mention because of their contribution to our fund of knowledge from which this book is partially derived. They are Curt Stein, M.D., Josh Mann, M.D., Anjum Khurshid, Ph.D., and Jennifer Andrews, M.S.

Most especially we thank Sheetal Malhotra, MBBS, MS, for her days and days of intense working making sure all our references in the final edition are as current and correct as possible.

Financial support for this project provided by members of the Board of Directors of The Medical Institute allowed this project to become reality. Without the help of the DEW Foundation and others this book would not have happened.

The unflagging encouragement and support of our long-time board chairman, Dr. Tom Fitch, has been not only appreciated but vital to our completion of this project.

Andrew McGuire at Moody Publishers has shepherded the process of taking this book from a mere sheaf of papers to the book you hold in your hands. His recommendations, suggestions, edits, and most importantly his driving force in putting all the parts together that are necessary for a book to happen were truly professional and unrelenting.

Pam Pugh, editor of this book, has added the perfection that a book based on science but written to be understood by the parents, mentors, and others concerned with the welfare of our children deserve. Thank you, Pam.

Our spouses have put up with us for years. We love them with all our hearts. Their tolerance with us for the hours we spent huddled over our computers in our separate homes being blithely unaware of what was going on around us is just one other example of the undeserved love that has been a core of the relationship each of us has had in our marriages. We thank you, Marion and Lee, with all our hearts and with all our love. You have us "hooked" and we are glad of it.

Joe S. McIlhaney, Jr., M.D.
and Freda McKissic Bush, M.D.

NOTES

The information in this book is derived from sources that include personal interviews, research journals, newspaper and news periodical reports, and books.

Chapter 1: Let's Talk Sex

1. William A. Marshall and J. M. Tanner, "Chapter 8: Puberty," in Falkner, F. Tanner, J. M., eds.: *Human Growth: A Comprehensive Treatise* 2nd ed. (New York: Plenum Publishing, 1986), 171–209.

2. Thomas R. Eng and William T. Butler, eds., *The Hidden Epidemic: Confronting Sexually Transmitted Disease* (Washington, D.C.: National Academy Press, 1997).

3. P. F. Horan, J. Phillips, and N. Hagen, "The Meaning of Abstinence for College Students," *Journal of HIV/AIDS Prevention and Education for Adolescents and Children* 2, no. 2 (1998): 51–66.

4. D. Kellock, C. P. O'Mahoney, "Sexually acquired metronidazole-resistant trichomoniasis in a lesbian couple," *Genitourinary Medicine,* 1996: 0172(1), 60–61.

5. Barbara Strauch, *The Primal Teen* (New York: Random House, 2003), 142.

6. Ibid., 143.

7. U. D. Upadhyay, M. J. Hindin, "Do perceptions of friends' behaviors affect age at first sex? Evidence from Cebu, Philippines," *Journal of Adolescent Health,* Oct. 2006: 39(4):570–7.

   R. E. Sieving, M. E. Eisenberg, S. Pettingell, C. Skay, "Friends' influence on adolescents' first sexual intercourse," *Perspectives on Sexual and Reproductive Health,* March 2006: 38(1):13–9.

8. R. E. Rector, K. A. Johnson, and L. R. Noyes, "Sexually Active Teenagers Are More Likely to Be Depressed and to Attempt Suicide," Washington, D.C.: A report from the Heritage Center for Data Analysis, The

Heritage Foundation. Publication CDA03–04, June 2 (2005).

D. D. Hallfors, M. W. Waller., C. A. Ford., C. T. Halpern, P. H. Brodesh, and B. Iritani, "Adolescent Depression and Suicide Risk-Association with Sex and Drug Behavior," *American Journal of Preventive Medicine* 27, no. 3 (2004): 224–231.

A. M. Meier, "Adolescent First Sex and Subsequent Mental Health," *American Journal of Sociology* 6 (2007): 112.

L. A. Shrier, S. K. Harris, and W. R. Beardslee, "Temporal Associations Between Depressive Symptoms and Self-Reported Sexually Transmitted Disease among Adolescents," *Archives of Pediatrics and Adolescent Medicine* 156 (June 2002): 599–606.

9. R. Finger, T. Thelen, J. Vessey, J. Mohn, and J. Mann, "Association of Virginity at Age 18 with Educational, Economic, Social, and Health Outcomes in Middle Adulthood," *Adolescent and Family Health* 3, no. 4 (2004): 164–170.

10. Ibid.

11. E. Laumann, R. T. Michael, G. Kolata, *Sex in America: A Definitive Survey* (New York: Time Warner, 1995), 125.

12. Peter Jensen as quoted in Barbara Strauch, *The Primal Teen*, 34–35.

13. Peter L. Benson, et al., "Hardwired to Connect: The New Scientific Case for Authoritative Communities," Commission on Children at Risk. Institute for American Values, (2003): 24–25.

Chapter 2: Meet the Brain

1. Glen Norval and Elizabeth Marquardt, principle investigators, "Hooking Up, Hanging Out, and Hoping for Mr. Right: College Women on Dating and Mating Today," Institute for American Values Report to the Independent Women's Forum, Institute for American Values (2001), 36–41.

2. Linda J. Waite and Kara Joyner, "Emotional and Physical Satisfaction in Married, Cohabiting, and Dating Sexual Unions: Do Men and Women Differ?" in *Studies on Sex*, eds., E. Laumann and R. Michael (Chicago: Univ. of Chicago, 1999).

3. J. N. Giedd, M.D., J. Blumenthal, N. O. Jeffries, F. X. Castellanos, H. Liu, A. Zijdenbos, T. Paus, A. C. Evans, and J. L. Rapoport, "Brain Development During Childhood and Adolescence: A Longitudinal MRI Study," *Nature Neuroscience* 2, no. 10 (1999): 861–863.

4. M. M. Ter-Pogossian, M. E. Phelps, and E. J. Hoffman, "A Positron-Emission Transaxial Tomography for Nuclear Imaging (PETT)," *Radiology* 114, no. 1 (1975): 89–98.

S. W. Kim, et al., "Brain activation by visual erotic stimuli in healthy middle aged males," *International Journal of Impotence Research*, Sept–Oct 2006: 18(5):452–7.

B. A. Arnow, J. E. Desmond, L. L. Banner, G. H. Glover, A. Solomon, M. L. Polan, T. F. Lue, S. W. Atlas, "Brain activation and sexual arousal in healthy, heterosexual males," *Brain*, May 2002: 125(Pt 5):1014–23.

5. Daniel R. Weinberger, M.D., Brita Elvevåg, Ph.D., and Jay N. Giedd, M.D., "The Adolescent Brain: A Work in Progress," The National Campaign to Prevent Teen Pregnancy (June 2005): 6–8.

6. Ibid.

7. J. Elman, E. A. Bates, M. Johnson, A. Karmiloff-Smith, D. Parisi, and K. Plunkett, *Rethinking Innateness: A Connectionist Perspective on Development* (Cambridge, MA: MIT Press, 1997).

8. Weinberger, Elvevåg, Giedd, 12.

9. Betty Birner, "Why Do Some People Have an Accent?" 2008 Linguistic Society of America, Washington, D.C., www.lsadc.org/info/ling-faqs-accent.cfm; *Science* 3, no 2 (2002): 115–36.

10. Charles A. Nelson, "Neural Plasticity and Human Development: The Role of Early Experience in Sculpting Memory Systems," *Current Directions in Psychological Science* (2000): 8(2): 42–45.

11. O. Arias-Carrion, E. Pöppel, "Dopamine, Learning and Reward-Seeking Behavior," *Acta Neurobiologiae Experimentalis* 67, no. 4 (2007): 481–488.

12. Linda P. Spear, "The Adolescent Brain and Age-Related Behavioral Manifestations," *Neuroscience and Biobehavioral Reviews* 24 (2000) 4: 424–25.

13. Barbara Strauch, *The Primal Teen* (New York: Random, 2003), 94.

14. Spear, "The Adolescent Brain and Age-Related Behavioral Manifestations," *Neuroscience and Biobehavioral Reviews* 24 (2000) 4: 424–425.

15. Michael D. De Bellis, M.D. et al., "Hippocampal Volume in Adolescent-Onset Alcohol Use Disorders," *American Journal of Psychiatry* 157 (2000): 737–744.

16. Spear, "The Adolescent Brain and Age-Related Behavioral Manifestations," *Neuroscience and Biobehavioral Reviews* 24 (2000) 4: 424–425.

17. Barbara Strauch, *The Primal Teen* (New York: Random, 2003), 94–95.

18. Louann Brizendine, M.D., *The Female Brain* (New York: Broadway, 2006), 37.

19. Peter L. Benson et al., "Hardwired to Connect: The New Scientific Case for Authoritative Communities," Commission on Children at Risk. Institute for American Values (2003): 16. Institute is not a journal, this is a published report.

20. 20. K. Uvnäs-Moberg, "Oxytocin May Mediate the Benefits of Positive Social Interaction and Emotions," *Psychoneuroendocrinology* (1998) 23(8):819–35.

J. L. Pawluski and L. A. Galea, "Hippocampal Morphology Is Differentially Affected by Reproductive Experience in the Mother," *Journal of*

Neurobiology 66, no. 1 (2006): 71–81.

21. H. Fisher, *Why We Love: The Nature and Chemistry of Romantic Love* (New York: Henry Holt, 2004).

22. Linda Waite and Maggie Gallagher, *The Case for Marriage: Why Married People are Happier, Healthier, and Better off Financially* (New York: Doubleday, 2000), 91.

23. Brizendine, MD., *The Female Brain,* 111.

24. Naomi I. Eisenberger and Matthew D. Lieberman, "Why Rejection Hurts: A Common Neural Alarm System for Physical and Social Pain" *Trends in Cognitive Sciences* 8, no. 7 (2004): 294–300.

25. Brizendine, MD., *The Female Brain,* 70–71.

26. Brizendine, MD., *The Female Brain,* 68.

    K. Grammar, (1993), "Androstadienone—a male pheromone?" *Ethology and Sociobiology* 14:201–7.

    M. K. McClintock, S. Bullivant, et al. (2005), "Human body scents: conscious perceptions and biological effects," *Chemical Senses* 30 (supplement 1): i135–i137.

27. Eisenberger and Lieberman, "Why Rejection Hurts."

28. J. F. Leckman and L. C. Mayes, "Preoccupations and Behaviors Associated with Romantic and Parental Love: Perspectives on the Origin of Obsessive-Compulsive Disorder," *Child and Adolescent Psychiatric Clinics of North America* 8, no. 3 (1999): 635–65.

29. Ibid.

30. Ibid.

31. A. Aron, H. Fisher, et al., (2005), "Reward, motivation, and emotional systems associated with early-stage intense romantic love," *Journal of Neurophysiology* 94 (1): 327–37.

32. Leckman and Mayes, "Preoccupations and Behaviors Associated with Romantic and Parental Love."

33. J. R. Kahn, K. A. London, "Premarital Sex and the Risk of Divorce," *Journal of Marriage and the Family* 53 (November 1991): 845–855.

    T. B. Heaton, "Factors Contributing to Increasing Marital Stability in the United States," *Journal of Family Issues*, Vol. 23 No. 3, April 2002, 392–409.

34. M. K. McClintock, S. Bullivant, et al., "Human Body Scents: Conscious Perceptions and Biological Effects," *Chemical Senses* 30, suppl. 1 (2005): i135–i137.

35. J. Havlicek, S. C. Roberts, J. Flegr, "Women's Preference for Dominant Male Odour: Effects of Menstrual Cycle and Relationship Status," *Biology Letters* (2005) 1(3):256–9.

    K. Grammer, B. Fink, N. Neave, "Human Pheromones and Sexual Attraction, *European Journal of Obstetrics & Gynecology and Reproductive*

Biology (2005) 1;118(2):135–42.

Chapter 3: The Developing Brain and Sex

1. M. Ernst, S.C. Mueller, "The Adolescent Brain: Insights from Functional Neuroimaging Research," Developmental Neurobiology (March 2008) 28;68(6):729–43.

2. Serge Stoleru et al., "Neuroanatomical Correlates of Visually Evoked Sexual Arousal in Human Males," *Archives of Sexual Behavior* 28 (1999): 1–21.

3. J. N. Giedd, M.D., J. Blumenthal, N. O. Jeffries, F. X. Castellanos, H. Liu, A. Zijdenbos, T. Paus, A. C. Evans, and J. L. Rapoport, "Brain Development during Childhood and Adolescence: A Longitudinal MRI Study," *Nature Neuroscience* 2, no. 10 (1999): 861–863.

4. Phineas Gage, "A Case for All Reasons," in C. Code, C. W. Wallesch, A. R. Lecours, and Y. Joanette, eds., *Classic Cases in Neuropsychology* (East Sussex, UK: M. Macmillan, 1996), 243–262.

5. John Mayer and Peter Salovey, "Social Intelligence," in Christopher Peterson and Martin Seligman, eds., *Character Strengths and Virtues: A Handbook and Classification* (New York: Oxford Univ. Press, 2004).

6. E. R. Sowell et al., "In Vivo Evidence for Post-Adolescent Brain Maturation in Frontal and Striatal Regions," *Nature Neuroscience* 2, no. 10 (1999): 859–861.

   Linda P. Spear, "The Adolescent Brain and Age-Related Behavioral Manifestations," *Neuroscience and Biobehavioral Reviews* 24 (2000): 424–425.

7. Giedd et al., "Brain Development During Childhood and Adolescence."

8. Q. Q. Sun, "The Missing Piece in the 'Use It or Lose It' Puzzle: Is Inhibition Regulated by Activity or Does It Act on Its Own Accord?" *Reviews Neuroscience* 18, nos. 3–4. (2007): 295–310.

9. Michael Resnick, "Best Bets for Improving the Odds for Optimum Youth Development," Commission on Children at Risk, *Working Paper* 10 (New York: Institute for American Values, 2002): 13.

   Michael Resnick et al., "The Impact of Caring and Connectedness on Adolescent Health and Well-Being," *Journal of Pediatrics and Child Health* 29 (1993): 1–9.

   V. Strasburger, "Clueless: why do pediatricians underestimate the media's influence on children and adolescents?" *Pediatrics*, April 2006: 117(4):1427–31.

10. Bureau of the Census, "Statistical Abstract of the United States: 2001" (Washington, D.C.: Governmental Printing Office, 2001): Table no. 258.

    Elizabeth M. Ozer et al., *America's Adolescents: Are They Healthy?* (San Francisco: National Adolescent Health Information Center, 2003), 37.

11. R. A. Turner, B. Januszewski, A. Flack, L. Guerin, B. Cooper, "Attachment

Representations and Sexual Behavior in Humans," *Annals of the New York Academy of Sciences* 1997;807:583–86.

B. Albert, S. Brown, C. M. Flanigan, eds., "14 and Younger: The Sexual Behavior of Young Adolescents: Summary," Washington, DC: National Campaign to Prevent Teen Pregnancy; 2003.

12. B. Albert, S. Brown, C. M. Flanigan, eds., "14 and Younger: The Sexual Behavior of Young Adolescents: Summary." Washington, DC: National Campaign to Prevent Teen Pregnancy; 2003.

    R. E. Rector, K. A. Johnson, L. R. Noyes, and S. Martin, *The Harmful Effects of Early Sexual Activity and Multiple Sexual Partners Among Women: A Book of Charts* (Washington, D.C: The Heritage Foundation, 2003), 1.

13. Brizendine, MD., *The Female Brain*, 68.

14. Martin K. Whyte, *Dating, Mating, and Marriage* (Edison, NJ: Aldine Transaction, 1990), 175–267.

    T. B. Heaton, "Factors Contributing to Increasing Marital Stability in the United States," *Journal of Family Issues* 23, no. 3 (2002): 392–409.

    J. H. Larson and T. B. Holman, "Premarital Predictors of Marital Quality and Stability," *Family Relations* 43 (1994): 228–236.

15. Norval Glenn and Elizabeth Marquardt, principle investigators, "Hooking Up, Hanging Out, and Hoping for Mr. Right: College Women on Dating and Mating Today," Institute for American Values Report to the Independent Women's Forum (2001), 20–21.

16. Bartels and Zeki, "The Neural Basis of Romantic Love," *Neuroreport* 11, no. 17 (2000): 3829–34.

17. Robert G. Bringle and Bram P. Buunk, "Extradyadic Relationships and Sexual Jealousy," in *Sexuality in Close Relationships*, eds. K. McKinney and S. Sprecher (Hillsdale, N.J.: Lawrence Erlbaum Associates, 1991), 135–53.

18. Daniel Goleman, *Social Intelligence* (New York: Bantam, 2006), 192.

19. C. S. Carter, "Neuroendocrine Perspectives on Social Attachment and Love," *Psychoneuroendocrinology* 23, no. 8 (1998): 779–818.

20. Eisenberger and Lieberman, "Why Rejection Hurts."

21. Naomi I. Eisenberger and Matthew D. Lieberman, "Why Rejection Hurts: A Common Neural Alarm System for Physical and Social Pain," *Trends Cogn Sci* 8, no. 7 (2004): 294–300.

22. J. Budziszewski, "Designed for Sex: What We Lose When We Forget What Sex Is For," *Touchstone* (July/August 2005): 22–27.

23. Serge Stoleru et al., "Neuroanatomical Correlates of Visually Evoked Sexual Arousal in Human Males," *Archives of Sexual Behavior* 28 (1999): 1–21.

    Rauch et al., "Neural Activation during Sexual and Competitive Arousal in Healthy Men," *Psychiatry Research* 91 (1999): 1–10.

24. Peter L. Benson et al., "Hardwired to Connect: The New Scientific Case for Authoritative Communities," Commission on Children at Risk, Institute for American Values (2003), 19.

25. Norval and Marquardt, "Hooking Up, Hanging Out, and Hoping for Mr. Right."

26. Allan N. Schore, *Affect Dysregulation and Disorders of the Self: The Neurobiology of Emotional Development* (New York: W. W. Norton & Co., 2003), xv.

    Schore, *Affect Regulation and the Origin of the Self: The Neurobiology of Emotional Development* (Hillsdale, N. J.: Lawrence Eribaum, 1994).

    Schore, *Affect Regulation and Repair of the Self: The Neurobiology of Emotional Development* (New York: W. W. Norton & Co., 2003).

27. R. Johnson, K. Browne, C. Hamilton-Giachritsis, "Young Children in Institutional Care at Risk of Harm," *Trauma Violence Abuse* 7, no. 1 (January 2006): 34–60.

28. Benedict Carey, "Shaping the Connection: Studies Renew Interest in Effects of the Parent-Child Bond," *Los Angeles Times*, March 31, 2003.

29. Allan N. Schore, *Affect Dysregulation and Disorders of the Self.*

30. Giacomo Rizzolatti, "The Mirror Neuron System and Its Function in Humans," *Annual Review of Neuroscience* Vol. 27: 169–192 (July 2004).

31. Daniel Goleman, *Emotional Intelligence* (New York: Bantam, 1997), 42.

32. Sarah Blaffer Hrdy, *Mother Nature: A History of Mothers, Infants, and Natural Selection* (New York: Pantheon, 1999), 393.

33. Allan N. Schore, *Affect Dysregulation and Disorders of the Self: The Neurobiology of Emotional Development* (New York: W.W. Norton and Co., 2003): xv.

    Schore, *Affect Regulation and the Origin of the Self: The Neurobiology of Emotional Development* (Hillsdale, N.J.: Lawrence Eribaum, 1994).

    Schore, *Affect Regulation and Repair of the Self: The Neurobiology of Emotional Development* (New York: W.W. Norton and Co., 2003).

34. Carol Platt Liebau, *Prude* (New York: Center Street, 2007), 165.

35. Martha K. McClintock and Gilbert Herdt, "Rethink Puberty: The Development of Sexual Attraction," *Human Development* 5, no. 6 (December 1996).

36. *Journal of Neurophysiology*, 94:327–37 (2005), 5/31/05.

    Edward Laumann, Robert T. Michael, and Gina Kolata, *Sex in America* (New York, Time Warner, 1995), 124.

37. Laumann et al., *Sex in America,* 97.

    Christine Bachrach, "Cohabitation and Reproductive Behavior in the U.S.," *Demography* 24, no. 4 (1987): 623–37.

38. L. W. Turner, S. S. Sizer, E. N. Whitney, and B. B. Wilks, *Life Choices:*

Health Concepts and Strategies, 2nd ed. (St. Paul, MN: West Publishing, 1992). Laumann et al., *Sex in America*, 124.

39. Edward Laumann et al., *Sex in America*, 88.

   Catherine E. Ross, John Mirowsky, and Karen Goldsteen, "The Impact of the Family on Health: Decade in Review," *Journal of Marriage and the Family* 52 (1990): 1061.

40. Barbara Strauch, *The Primal Teen* (New York: Random House, 2003), 147.

41. D. Marazziti and D. Canale, "Hormonal Changes When Falling in Love," *Psychoneuroendocrinology* 29, no. 7 (August 2004): 931–6.

42. A. Bartels and S. Zeki, "The Neural Basis of Romantic Love," Neuroreport 11(17), 3829–34.

43. Michael R. Cunningham et al., "Social Allergies in Romantic Relationships: Behavioral Repetition, Emotional Sensitization, and Dissatisfaction in Dating Couples," *Personal Relationships* 12 (2005): 273–95.

44. A. Bartels, S. Zeki, "The Neural Basis of Romantic Love," *Neuroreport* (2000) 11 (17) 3829–34.

45. R. E. Rector, K. A. Johnson, L. R. Noyes, and S. Martin, *The Harmful Effects of Early Sexual Activity and Multiple Sexual Partners Among Women: A Book of Charts* (Washington, D.C.: The Heritage Foundation, 2003).

46. C. S. Carter, "Neuroendocrine Perspectives on Social Attachment and Love," *Psychoneuroendocrinology* 23, no. 8 (1998): 779–818.

47. Aron et al., "Reward, Motivation, and Emotion Systems Associated with Early-Stage Intense Romantic Love," *Journal of Neurophysiology* (2005) 94:327–37.

48. Janice K. Kiecolt-Glaser et al., "Psychoneuroimmunology: Psychological Influences on Immune Function and Health," *Journal of Consulting and Clinical Psychology* 70, no. 3 (2002): 537–547.

49. William B. Malarkey et al., "Hostile Behavior during Marital Conflict Alters Pituitary and Adrenal Hormones," *Psychosomatic Medicine* 56 (1994): 41–51.

50. J. A. Coan et al., "Spouse, but not stranger: hand-holding attenuates activation in neural systems underlying response to threat," *Psychophysiology* 42 (2005), S44.

51. Arthur Aron et al., "Reward, Motivation, and Emotion Systems Associated with Early-Stage Intense Romantic Love," *Journal of Neurophysiology* 94 (2005): 327–337.

52. Serge Stoleru et al., "Neuroanatomical Correlates of Visually Evoked Sexual Arousal In Human Males," *Archives of Sexual Behavior* 28 (1999): 1–21.

53. J. Budziszewski, "Designed for Sex: What We Lose When We Forget What Sex Is For," *Touchstone* (July/August 2005): 22–27.

54. Dave Carder, *Close Calls* (Chicago: Moody, 2008), 23.

Chapter 4: Baggage Claim

1. L. Koenig, L. Doll, A. O'Leary, and W. Pequegnat, *From Child Sexual Abuse to Adult Sexual Risk-Trauma, Revictimization, and Intervention.* Washington, DC: American Psychological Association, 2004, 4.

2. L. F. Salazar et al., "Biologically Confirmed Sexually Transmitted Infection and Depressive Symptomatology among African-American Female Adolescents," *Sexually Transmitted Infection* (February 2006) Vol. 82, 55–60.

3. Peggy Brick, M. Ed. et al., *Guidelines for Comprehensive Sexuality Education*, 3rd. ed. (New York: The Sexuality Information and Education Council of the United States, 2004), 17, 19–20, 52–53, 71.

4. Meg Meeker, *Epidemic: How Teen Sex is Killing Our Kids* (Washington, DC: LifeLine Press, 2002), 26–29.

5. J. L. H. Evers, "Female Subfertility," *Lancet* (2002): 360(9327):151–59.

6. Centers for Disease Control and Prevention, J. A. Grunbaum, L. Kann, S. A. Kinchen, et al., "Youth Risk Behavior Surveillance—United States 2001," *Morbidity and Mortality Weekly Report: Surveillance Summary* 51, no. 4 (2002).

7. Centers for Disease Control and Prevention, "Youth Risk Behavior Surveillance: National College Health Risk Behavior Survey—United States, 1995," *Morbidity and Mortality Weekly Report Surveillance Summary* 46, no. 6 (November 14, 1997): 1–56.

8. W. D. Mosher, A. Chandra, J. Jones, "Sexual Behavior and Selected Health Measures: Men and Women 15–44 Years of Age, United States, 2002 ." Advance data from vital and health statistics; no 362. Hyattsville, MD: National Center for Health Statistics, 2005.

9. Glenn Norval and Elizabeth Marquardt, *Hooking up, Hanging Out, and Hoping for Mr. Right: College Women on Dating and Mating Today* (New York: Institute for American Values, 2002), 4.

10. A. Chandra, G. M. Martinez, W. D. Mosher, J. C. Abma, J. Jones, "Fertility, family planning, and reproductive health of U.S. women: Data from the 2002 National Survey of Family Growth," National Center for Health Statistics, *Vital and Health Statistics* 23(25), 2005.

11. R. E. Rector, K. A. Johnson, L. R. Noyes, and S. Martin, *The Harmful Effects of Early Sexual Activity and Multiple Sexual Partners among Women: A Book of Charts* (Washington, DC: The Heritage Foundation, 2003), 4.

12. R. A. Turner, B. Januszewski, A. Flack, L. Guerin, and B. Cooper, "Attachment Representations and Sexual Behavior in Humans," *Annals of the New York Academy of Science*, vol. 807 (1997): 583–586.

13. Ibid.

14. K. Uvnas-Moberg, *The Oxytocin Factor* (New York: Perseus Books, 2003).

15. N. I. Eisenberger and M. D. Lieberman, "Why rejection hurts: A common neural alarm system for physical and social pain," *Trends in Cognitive Science* (2004): 8 (7): 294–300.

16. Peter L. Benson, et al., "Hardwired to Connect: The New Scientific Case for Authoritative Communities," Commission on Children at Risk. Institute for American Values (2003), 16–17.

17. Robert T. Michael, John H. Gagnon, Edward Laumann, Gina Kolata, *Sex in America* (Time Warner, 1995), page 124.

18. R. E. Rector, K. A. Johnson, and L. R. Noyes, "Sexually Active Teenagers Are More Likely to Be Depressed and to Attempt Suicide," Washington, DC: The Heritage Center for Data Analysis, The Heritage Foundation, Publication CDA03-04, 6/3/2003.

19. The American College Health Association, National College Health Assessment, Spring 2006, http://www.acha-ncha.org/.

20. B. Albert, S. Brown, and C. M. Flanigan, eds., "14 and Younger: The Sexual Behavior of Young Adolescents" (Washington, D.C. National Campaign to Prevent Teen Pregnancy, 2003).

21. N. I. Eisenberger and M. D. Lieberman, "Why Rejection Hurts: A Common Neural Alarm System for Physical and Social Pain," *Trends in Cognitive Science* 8, no. 7 (2004): 294–300.

22. Lydia A. Shrier, M.D., M.P.H.; Sion Kim Harris, Ph.D.; William R. Beardslee, M.D., "Temporal Associations Between Depressive Symptoms and Self-Reported Sexually Transmitted Disease Among Adolescents," Archives of Pediatric and Adolescent Medicine, Vol. 156, June 2002: 599–605.

23. J. McIlhaney, *Sex: What You Don't Know Can Kill You* (Ada, MI: Baker, 1997), 95.

24. T. B. Heaton, "Factors Contributing to Increasing Marital Stability in the United States," *Journal of Family Issues* 23, no. 3 (2002): 392–409.

    S. S. Janus and C. L. Janus, *The Janus Report on Human Sexuality* (New York: Wiley, 1993), 175–176.

    J. R. Kahn and K. A. London, "Reply to Comment on Kahn and London," *Journal of Marriage and Family* 55 (1991): 241.

25. Kahn, J.R. and K. A. London, "Reply to Comment on Kahn and London," *Journal of Marriage and Family* 55 (1991): 241.

26. *Tracking the Hidden Epidemics 2000: Trends in STDs in the United States* (Atlanta, GA: Centers for Disease Control and Prevention, U.S. Dept. of Health and Human Services, 2000).

27. H. Weinstock, S. Berman, and W. Cates, Jr., "Sexually Transmitted Diseases among American Youth: Incidence and Prevalence Estimates, 2000," *Perspectives on Sexual and Reproductive Health* 36, no. 1 (2004): 6–10.

28. R. J. DiClemente, R. A. Crosby, G. M. Wingood, D. L. Lang, L. F. Salazar, S. D. Broadwell, "Reducing risk exposures to zero and not having multiple partners: findings that inform evidence-based practices designed to prevent STD acquisition," *International Journal of STD and AIDS* (Dec. 2005);16(12):816–8.

29. Freda Bush, M.D., personal notes.

30. R. L. Coley and P. L. Chase-Lansdale, "Adolescent Pregnancy and Parenthood: Recent Evidence and Future Directions," *American Psychologist* 53, no. 2 (1998): 152–166.

31. Annie E. Casey Foundation, *When Teens Have Sex: Issues and Trends* (Baltimore, MD: Annie E. Casey Foundation, 1998).

32. R. A. Maynard, ed., "Kids Having Kids: A Robin Hood Foundation Special Report on the Costs of Adolescent Child Bearing" (New York, NY: Robin Hood Foundation, 1996), 18.

33. Annie E. Casey Foundation, *When Teens Have Sex: Issues and Trends.*

34. U.S. Congressional Budget Office, *Sources of Support for Adolescent Mothers* (Washington, DC: CBO Publications Office, 1990).

35. Ibid.

36. R. A. Maynard, ed., "Kids Having Kids: A Robin Hood Foundation Special Report on the Costs of Adolescent Child Bearing" (New York, NY: Robin Hood Foundation, 1996).

37. J. E. Darroch, D. J. Landry, S. Oslak, "Age differences between sexual partners in the U.S.," *Family Planning Perspectives* (1999); 31(4): 160–67.

38. Centers for Disease Control and Prevention. "Youth Risk Behavior Surveillance: National College Health Risk Behavior Survey—United States, 1995."

39. L. M. Dinerman, M. D. Wilson, A. K. Duggan, and A. Joffe, "Outcomes of Adolescents Using Levonorgestrel Implants vs. Oral Contraceptives or Other Contraceptive Methods," *Archives of Pediatric and Adolescent Medicine* 149, no 9 (1995): 967–972.

40. Haishan Fu, Jacqueline E. Darroch, Taylor Haas, and Nalini Ranjit, "Contraceptive Failure Rates: New Estimates From the 1995 National Survey of Family Growth," *Family Planning Perspectives* (March/April 1999): 31(2).

41. R. A. Hatcher, J. Trussell, and F. Stewart, et al., eds., *Contraceptive Technology*, 18th rev. ed. (New York, NY: Ardent Media, 2004).

42. Ibid.

44. C. E. Irwin, Jr., "Risk taking behaviors in the adolescent patient: Are they impulsive?" *Pediatric Annals* 18 (1989): 122–33.

44. "Fertility, Family Planning, and Women's Health; New Data from the 1995 National Survey of Family Growth," *Vital and Health Statistics* 23, no. 19 (Centers for Disease Control and Prevention, May 1997).

45. C. Pacifici, M. Stoolmiler, C. Nelson, "Evaluating a Prevention Program for Teenagers on Sexual Coercion: a Differential Effectiveness Program," *Journal of Consulting Clinical Psychologists* (2001) 69:552–9.

M. Blythe, D. Fortenberry, M. Temkit, et al., "Incidence and Correlates of Unwanted Sex in Relationships in Middle and Late Adolescent Women, *Archives of Pediatric Adolescent Medicine* (2005) 160:591–5.

46. B. Albert, S. Brown, and C. M. Flanigan, eds., "14 and Younger: The Sexual Behavior of Young Adolescents: Summary," (Washington, DC: National Campaign to Prevent Teen Pregnancy, 2003).

47. Centers for Disease Control and Prevention, "Understanding Sexual Violence" Fact Sheet, 2007. Available online at: http://www.cdc.gov/ncipc/pubres/images/SV%20Factsheet.pdf.

48. Oliver Berton et al., "Essential Role of BDNF in Mesolimbic Dopamine Pathway in Social Defeat Stress," *Science* (February 2006): 311, 864–868.

49. L. K. Van Bruggen, M. G. Runtz, H. Kadlec, "Sexual revictimization: the role of sexual self-esteem and dysfunctional sexual behaviors," *Child Maltreatment* (May 2006): 11(2):131–45.

50. *Mental Health: A Report of the Surgeon General* (Rockville, MD; U. S. Department of Health and Human Services, Substance Abuse and Mental Health Services Administration, Center for Mental Health Services, National Institutes of Health, National Institute of Mental Health, 1999): Tables 2–7.

L. Koenig, L. Doll, A. O'Leary, and W. Pequegnat, "From Child Sexual Abuse to Adult Sexual Risk," (Washington, DC: American Psychological Association 2003): 4–5.

51. Koenig et al., "From Child Sexual Abuse to Adult Sexual Risk," 33, 37.

52. K. A. Kendall-Tackett, L. M. Williams, and D. Finkelhor, "Impact of Sexual Abuse on Children: A Review and Synthesis of Recent Empirical Studies," *Psychology Bulletin* 113, no. 1 (January 1993): 164–0.

53. L. J. Cohen, K. Nikiforov, S. Gans, O. Poznansky, P. McGeoch, C. Weaver, E. G. King, K. Cullen, I. Galynker, "Heterosexual male perpetrators of childhood sexual abuse: a preliminary neuropsychiatric model," *Psychiatric Quarterly* (Winter 2002): 73(4):313–36.

M. F. Mendez, T. Chow, J. Ringman, G. Twitchell, C. H. Hinkin, "Pedophilia and temporal lobe disturbances," *Journal of Neuropsychiatry and Clinical Neuroscience* (Winter 2000): 12(1):71-6.

54. "In the Mind of a Predator," *Austin-American Statesman* (2005).

55. J. Smolowe, "Sex With a Scorecard: A Group of High School Boys Who Tallied Their Conquests Ignites a Debate over Teenage Values," *Time Magazine* (April 5, 1993).

http://www.time.com/time/magazine/article/0,9171,978157,00.html

56. E. J. Kanin, "Date-rapists: differential sexual socialization and relative depravation," *Archives of Sexual Behavior* 14 (1985), 219–231.

57. R. F. Valois, J. E. Oeltmann, J. Waller, J. R. Hussey, "Relationship Between Number of Sexual Intercourse Partners and Selected Health Risk Behaviors Among Public High School Adolescents," *Journal of Adolescent Health* (Nov. 1999): 25(5): 328–35.

58. B. Albert (2007), "With One Voice: America's Adults and Teens Sound Off About Teen Pregnancy," Washington, DC: National Campaign to Prevent Teen Pregnancy. Available online at https://www.teenpregnancy.org/product/pdf/6_9_2007_15_17_14WOV2007_fulltext.pdf.

59. L. J. Waite and M. Gallagher, *The Case for Marriage: Why Married People Are Happier, Healthier, and Better Off Financially* (New York: Doubleday, 2000), 128–140.

Chapter 5: Thinking Long-Term

1. Edward Laumann, Robert T. Michael, and Gina Kolata, *Sex in America* (New York: Time Warner, 1995), 97, 99.

2. Ibid.

3. Ibid., 105.

4. Ibid., 127.

5. J. R. Kahn and K. A. London, "Premarital Sex and the Risk of Divorce," *Journal of Marriage and the Family* 53 (November 1991): 845–855.

   T. B. Heaton, "Factors Contributing to Increasing Marital Stability in the United States," *Journal of Family Issues* 23, no. 3 (April 2002): 392–409.

6. R. Finger et al., "Association of Virginity at Age 18 with Educational, Economic, Social, and Health Outcomes in Middle Adulthood," *Adolescent and Family Health* 3, no. 4 (2004): 164–170.

7. L. J. Waite and M. Gallagher, *The Case for Marriage: Why Married People Are Happier, Healthier, and Better Off Financially* (New York: Doubleday, 2000), 36.

8. Laumann, Michael, and Kolata, *Sex in America*, 97–98.

9. Larry L. Bumpass, "The Declining Significance of Marriage: Changing Family Life in the United States." Paper presented at the Potsdam International Conference, "Changing Families and Childhood," December 14–17, 1994.

   Larry L. Bumpass and James A. Sweet, "National Estimates of Cohabitation," *Demography* 26 (1989): 615–625.

   D. T Lichter, Z. Qian, L.M. Mellott, "Marriage or dissolution? Union transitions among poor cohabiting women," *Demography* (May 2006): 43(2):223-40.

   Larry Bumpass, Hsien-Hen Lu, "Trends in Cohabitation and Implications for Children's Family Contexts in the United States," *Population Studies*, Vol. 54, No. 1 (Mar., 2000), 29–41.

10. Lee A. Lillard, Michael J. Brien, and Linda J. Waite, "Pre-Marital Cohabitation and Subsequent Marital Dissolution: Is It Self-Selection?" *Demography* 32 (1995): 437–458.

    Elizabeth Thomson and Ugo Collela, "Cohabitation and Marital Stability: Quality or Commitment?" *Journal of Marriage and the Family* 54 (1992): 259–268.

    G. K. Rhoades, S. M. Stanley, H. J. Markman, "Pre-engagement cohabitation and gender asymmetry in marital commitment," *Journal of Family Psychology* (Dec. 2006): 20(4):553–60.

11. Larry L. Bumpass, R. Kelly Raley, and James A. Sweet, "The Changing Character of Stepfamilies: Implications of Cohabitation and Nonmarital Childbearing," *Demography* 32: 425–436.

12. L. J. Waite and M. Gallagher, *The Case for Marriage*, 38.

13. C. T. Kenney, S. S. McLanahan, "Why are cohabiting relationships more violent than marriages?" *Demography* (Feb. 2006): 43(1):127–40.

14. Louanne Brizendine, M.D., *The Female Brain* (New York: Broadway, 2006), 72.

15. Marin Clarkberg, Ross M. Stolzenberg, and Linda J. Waite, "Attitudes, Values and Entrance in to Cohabitational Versus Marital Unions," *Social Forces* 4 (1995): 609–32.

16. Waite and Gallagher, *The Case for Marriage*, 39.

17. Linda J. Waite and Kara Joyner, "Emotional and Physical Satisfaction in Married, Cohabiting and Dating Sexual Unions: Do Men and Women Differ?" in *Studies on Sex*, E. Laumann and R. Michael, eds. (Chicago: Univ. of Chicago Press, 1995).

18. Waite and Gallagher, *The Case for Marriage*, 91.

    David M. Buss, *The Evolution of Desire: Strategies of Human Mating* (New York: Basic Books, 1994).

19. Waite and Gallagher, *The Case for Marriage*, 86.

20. Laumann, Michael, and Kolata, *Sex in America*, 75.

21. Ibid.,130.

22. J. R. Kahn and K. R. London, "Premarital Sex and the Risk of Divorce," *Journal of Marriage and the Family* 53 (November 1991): 845–855.

    T. B. Heaton, "Factors Contributing to Increasing Marital Stability in the United States," *Journal of Family Issues* 23, no. 3 (April 2002): 392–409.

    R. Whelan, "Broken Homes and Battered Children: A Study of the Relationship between Child Abuse and Family Type," a report by the Family Education Trust (1993): 29.

    M. D. Bramlett and W. D. Mosher, "Cohabitation, Marriage, Divorce, and Remarriage in the United States," *Vital Health Stat* 23, no. 22 (2002): 1–93.

23. Glenn Norval and Elizabeth Marquardt, *Hooking up, Hanging Out, and Hoping for Mr. Right: College Women on Dating and Mating Today*, Institute for American Values (2002), 13.

24. Centers for Disease Control and Prevention. Youth Risk Behavior Surveillance: United States, 2005, Surveillance Summaries, 2006. MMWR 2006; 55 (No. SS-5).

25. W. D. Mosher, S. Chandra, and J. Jones, "Sexual Behavior and Selected Health Measures: Men and Women 15–44 Years of Age" (2002). (Hyattsville, MD: National Center for Health Statistics, 2005). Advance Data from *Vital and Health Statistics*, no. 362.

26. Ibid.

27. Centers for Disease Control and Prevention. Youth Risk Behavior Surveillance: United States, 2005. Surveillance Summaries, 2006. MMWR 2006; 55 (No. SS-5).

28. Ibid.

29. American College Health Association, *National College Health Assessment* (Spring 2006).

30. Ibid.

31. Ibid.

32. T. B. Heaton, "Factors Contributing to Increasing Marital Stability in the United States," *Journal of Family Issues* 23, no. 3 (2002): 392–409.

Larry Bumpass, Hsien-Hen Lu, "Trends in Cohabitation and Implications for Children's Family Contexts in the United States," *Population Studies*, Vol. 54, No. 1 (Mar., 2000), 29–41.

J. R. Kahn, K. A. London, "Premarital Sex and the Risk of Divorce," *Journal of Marriage and the Family* 53 (November 1991): 845–855.

33. R. Finger et al., "Association of Virginity at Age 18 with Educational, Economic, Social, and Health Outcomes in Middle Adulthood," *Adolescent and Family Health* 3, no. 4 (2004): 164–170.

34. J. Budziszewski, "Designed for Sex," *Touchstone* (July/August 2005): 22–27.

35. *Guidelines for Comprehensive Sexuality Education*, 3rd ed., (The Sexuality Information and Education Council of the United States, 2004): 52–53.

36. P. Roger Hillerstrom and Karlyn Hillerstrom, *The Intimacy Cover-Up: Uncovering the Difference Between Love and Sex* (Grand Rapids, MI: Kregel, 2004), 29–31.

Allan Bloom, *The Closing of the American Mind* (New York: Simon & Schuster, 1987), 113.

37. L. T. Garcia, C. Markey, "Matching in sexual experience for married, cohabitating, and dating couples," *Journal of Sex Research* (Aug. 2007): 44(3):250–5.

38. B. Albert (2007), "With One Voice: America's Adults and Teens Sound Off About Teen Pregnancy," Washington, DC: National Campaign to Prevent Teen Pregnancy. Available at https://www.teenpregnancy.org/ product/pdf/6_9_2007_15_17_14WOV2007_fulltext.pdf.

39. Norman Doidge, M.D., *The Brain That Changes Itself* (New York: Viking, 2007). Excerpt from dust jacket material.

40. Sharon Begley, "When Does Your Brain Stop Making New Neurons?" *Newsweek* (July 2, 2007), 62.

    Marcia Barinaga, "New Leads to Brain Neuron Regeneration," *Science* vol. 282, no. 391 (November 1998): 1018–19.

41. M. Scott Peck, M.D., *The Road Less Traveled* (New York: Touchstone, 1978), 53.

Chapter 6: The Pursuit of Happiness

1. M. D. Resnick, P. S. Bearman, R. W. Blum, et al., "Protecting Adolescents from Harm: Findings from the National Longitudinal Study on Adolescent Health," *JAMA* 278, no. 10 (1997): 823–832.

   B. Albert (2007), "With One Voice: America's Adults and Teens Sound Off About Teen Pregnancy," Washington, DC: National Campaign to Prevent Teen Pregnancy. Available at https://www.teenpregnancy.org/ product/pdf/6_9_2007_15_17_14WOV2007_fulltext.pdf.

2. National Campaign to Prevention Teen Pregnancy, *With One Voice 2002: America's Adults and Teens Sound Off about Teen Pregnancy: An Annual National Survey* (Washington, D.C.: National Campaign to Prevention Teen Pregnancy, December 2002).

   Glenn Norval and Elizabeth Marquardt, *Hooking up, Hanging Out and Hoping for Mr. Right: College Women on Dating and Mating Today* (Washington, DC: Institute for American Values, 2002), 60.

3. C. McNeely, M. L. Shew, T. Beuhring, R. Sieving, B. C. Miller, and R. W. Blum, "Mothers' Influence on the Timing of First Sex among 14- and 15-Year-Olds," *Journal of Adolescent Health* 31, no. 3 (2002): 256–265.

4. D. J. Whitaker and K. S. Miller, "Parent-Adolescent Discussions about Sex and Condoms: Impact on Peer Influences of Sexual Risk Behavior," *Journal of Adolescent Research* 15, no. 2 (2000): 251–273.

   S. S. Feldman and D. A. Rosemthal, eds., *Talking Sexuality: Parent-Adolescent Communication: New Directions for Child and Adolescent Development* (San Francisco, CA: Jossey-Bass, 2002).

5. Judith S. Wallerstein and Sandra Blakeslee, *The Good Marriage: How and Why Love Lasts* (Boston: Houghton Mifflin, 1995).

6. Ibid.

7. J. N. Giedd, J. Blumenthal, N. O. Jeffries, F. X. Castellanos, H. Liu, A. Zijdenbos, T. Paus, A. C. Evans, and J. L. Rapoport, "Brain Development during Childhood and Adolescence: A Longitudinal MRI Study,"

Nature Neuroscience 2, no. 10 (1999): 861–863.

8. H. R. White, V. Johnson, and S. Buyske, "Parental Modeling and Parenting Behavior Effects on Offspring Alcohol and Cigarette Use: A Growth Curve Analysis," *Journal of Substance Abuse* 12, no. 3 (2000): 287–310.

   C. Li, M. A. Pentz, and C. P. Chou, "Parental Substance Use as a Modifier of Adolescent Substance Use Risk," *Addiction* 97, no. 12 (2002): 1537–1550.

   P. J. Dittus, J. Jaccard, "Adolescents' perceptions of maternal disapproval of sex: relationship to sexual outcomes," *Journal of Adolescent Health*, (2000): 26(4):268–78.

9. R. J. DiClemente, G. M. Wingood, R. Crosby, et al., "Parental monitoring: association with adolescents' risk behaviors," *Pediatrics* (2001): 107(6):1363–1368.

   J. G. Baker, S. L. Rosenthal, D. Leonhardt, et al., "Relationship between perceived parental monitoring and young adolescent girls' sexual and substance use behaviors," *Journal of Pediatric and Adolescent Gynecology* (1999): 12(1):17–22.

   L. Steinberg, A. Fletcher, N. Darling, "Parental monitoring and peer influences on adolescent substance use," *Pediatrics* (1994): 93(6 Pt. 2):1060–1064.

10. J. Jaccard, P. J. Dittus, and V. V. Gordon, "Parent-Teen Communication about Premarital Sex: Factors Associated with the Extent of Communication," *Journal of Adolescent Research* 15, no. 2 (2000): 187–208.

    S. S. Feldman and D. A. Rosemthal, eds., *Talking Sexuality: Parent-Adolescent Communication: New Directions for Child and Adolescent Development* (San Francisco, CA: Jossey-Bass, 2002).

11. Jaccard et al., "Parent-Teen Communication."

12. Ibid.

13. P. S. Karofsky, L. Zeng, and M. R. Kosorok, "Relationship between Adolescent-Parental Communication and Initiation of First Intercourse by Adolescents," *Journal of Adolescent Health* 28, no. 1 (2000): 41–45.

    M. D. Resnick, P. S. Bearman, R. W. Blum, et al., "Protecting Adolescents from Harm: Findings from the National Longitudinal Study on Adolescent Health," *Journal of the American Medical Association* 278, no. 10 (1997): 823–832.

    C. DiIorio, M. Kelley, and M. Hockenberry-Eaton, "Communication about Sexual Issues: Mothers, Fathers, and Friends," *Journal of Adolescent Health* 24, no. 3 (1999): 181–189.

14. R. P. Lederman, W. Chan, and C. Roberts-Gray, "Sexual Risk Attitudes and Intentions of Youth Aged 12–14 Years: Survey Comparisons of Parent-Teen Prevention and Control Groups," *Behavioral Medicine* 29, no. 4 (2004): 155–163.

15. P. J. Dittus and J. Jaccard, "Adolescents' Perceptions of Maternal Disapproval of Sex: Relationship to Sexual Outcomes," *Journal of Adolescent Health* 26, no. 4 (2000): 268–278.

   C. McNeely, M. L. Shew, T. Beuhring, R. Sieving, B. C. Miller, and R. W. Blum, "Mothers' Influence on the Timing of First Sex among 14- and 15-Year-Olds," *Journal of Adolescent Health* 31, no. 3 (2002): 256–65.

16. M. D. Resnick, P. S. Bearman, R. W. Blum, et al., "Protecting Adolescents from Harm: Findings from the National Longitudinal Study on Adolescent Health," *JAMA* 278, no. 10 (1997): 823–32.

17. J. Jaccard, P. J. Dittus, and V. V. Gordon, "Parent-Teen Communication about Premarital Sex: Factors Associated with the Extent of Communication," *Journal of Adolescent Research* 15, no. 2 (2000): 187–208.

18. H. R. White, V. Johnson, and S. Buyske, "Parental Modeling and Parenting Behavior Effects on Offspring Alcohol and Cigarette Use: A Growth Curve Analysis," *Journal of Substance Abuse* 12, no. 3 (2000): 287–310.

   C. Li, M. A. Pentz, and C. P. Chou, "Parental Substance Use as a Modifier of Adolescent Substance Use Risk," *Addiction* 97, no. 12 (2002): 1537–1550.

   P. J. Dittus, J. Jaccard, "Adolescents' perceptions of maternal disapproval of sex: relationship to sexual outcomes," *Journal of Adolescent Health* (2000): 26(4):268–78.

19. Thomas R. Eng and William T. Butler, eds., "The Hidden Epidemic," A report by the Committee on Prevention and Control for Sexually Transmitted Diseases, Institute of Medicine, National Academy Press, 1997.

20. H. Weinstock, S. Berman and W. Cates, Jr., "Sexually Transmitted Diseases among American Youth; Incidence and Prevelance Estimates, 2000," *Sex and Reproductive Health* 36 (2004): 6–10.

21. Peter L. Benson, et al., "Hardwired to Connect: The New Scientific Case for Authoritative Communities," Commission on Children at Risk. Institute for American Values (2003), 33.

22. M. L. Vincent, A. F. Clearie, and M. D. Schluchter, "Reducing Adolescent Pregnancy through School and Community-Based Education," *JAMA* 257, no. 24 (1987): 3382–3386.

   H. P. Koo, G. H. Dunterman, C. George, Y. Green, and M. L. Vincent, "Reducing Adolescent Pregnancy through a School- and Community-Based Intervention: Denmark, South Carolina, Revisited," *Family Planning Perspectives* 26, no. 5 (1994): 206–211, 217.

23. Centers for Disease Control and Prevention. Youth Risk Behavior Surveillance: National College Health Risk Behavior Survey—United States, 1995.

24. G. R. Donenberg, F. B. Bryant, E. Emerson, H. W. Wilson, and K. E. Pasch, "Tracing the Roots of Early Sexual Debut among Adolescents in Psychiatric Care," *Journal of the American Academy of Child Adolescent*

Psychiatry 42, no. 5 (2003): 594–608.

American Social Health Association, "Sex on the Brain: Peer Pressure." See www.iwannaknow.org.

25. C. Pacifici, M. Stoolmiler, and C. Nelson, "Evaluating a Prevention Program for Teenagers on Sexual Coercion: A Differential Effectiveness Program," *Journal of Consulting and Clinical Psychology* 69 (2001): 552–9.

M. Blythe, D. Fortenberry, and M. Temkit, et al., "Incidence and Correlates of Unwanted Sex in Relationships in Middle and Late Adolescent Women," *Arch Pediatr Adolesc Med* 160 (2005): 591–5.

26. Glenn Norval and Elizabeth Marquardt, *Hooking up, Hanging Out, and Hoping for Mr. Right: College Women on Dating and Mating Today* (Washington, DC: Institute for American Values, 2002), 14.

27. L. J. Waite and M. Gallagher, *The Case for Marriage: Why Married People Are Happier, Healthier, and Better Off Financially* (New York: Doubleday, 2000), 64.

M. R. Pergamit, L. Huang, and J. Lane, "The Long-Term Impact of Adolescent Risky Behaviors and Family Environment" (Chicago: National Opinion Research Center (NORC), Univ. of Chicago, August 2001).

28. M. D. Resnick, P. S. Bearman, R. W. Blum, et al., "Protecting Adolescents from Harm: Findings from the National Longitudinal Study on Adolescent Health," *JAMA* 278, no. 10 (1997): 823–832.

29. B. Albert, (2007), "With One Voice: America's Adults and Teens Sound Off About Teen Pregnancy." Washington, DC: National Campaign to Prevent Teen Pregnancy. Available at https://www.teenpregnancy.org/product/pdf/6_9_2007_15_17_14WOV2007_fulltext.pdf.

30. P. Haag, *Voices of a Generation: Teenage Girls on Sex, School, and Self* (Washington, D.C.: American Association of University Women Educational Foundation, 1999).

31. P. S. Bearman and H. Bruckner, "Promising the Future: Virginity Pledges and First Intercourse," *American Journal of Sociology*, vol. 106, no. 4 (2001): 859–912.

32. L. F. O'Sullivan and J. Brooks-Gunn, "The Timing of Changes in Girls' Sexual Cognition and Behaviors in Early Adolescence: A Prospective, Cohort Study," *Journal of Adolescent Health* 37, no. 3 (September 2005): 209–11.

33. American Social Health Association, "Sex on the Brain: Peer Pressure." See www.iwannaknow.org.

34. Ibid.

35. L. Harris, R. F. Oman, S. K. Vesely, E. L. Tolma, C. B. Aspy, S. Rodine, L. Marshall, and J. Fluhr, "Associations between Youth Assets and Sexual Activity: Does Adult Supervision Play a Role?" *Child Care Health Dev* 334, no. 4 (July 2007): 448–54.

36. Centers for Disease Control and Prevention. Youth Risk Behavior Sur-

veillance: United States, 2005. Surveillance Summaries, 2006. MMWR 2006; 55 (No. SS-5).

The National Center on Addiction and Substance Abuse at Columbia University, *Rethinking Rites of Passage: Substance Abuse on America's Campuses: A Report by the Commission on Substance Abuse at Colleges and Universities* (New York, NY: Columbia Univ., June 1994).

R. Lowry, D. Holtzman, B. I. Truman, L. Kann, J. L. Collins, and L. J. Kolbe, "Substance Use and HIV-Related Sexual Behaviors among U.S. High School Students: Are They Related?" *American Journal of Public Health* 84, no. 7 (1994): 1116–1120.

F. L. Mott, M. M. Fondell, P. N. Hu, L. Kowaleski-Jones, and E. G. Menaghan, "Determinants of First Sex by Age 14 in a High-Risk Adolescent Population," *Family Planning Perspectives* 28, no. 1 (1996): 13–18.

37. M. D. Resnick, P. S. Bearman, R. W. Blum, et al., "Protecting Adolescents from Harm: Findings from the National Longitudinal Study on Adolescent Health," *JAMA* 278, no. 10 (1997): 823–832.

38. C. S. Carter, "Neuroendocrine Perspectives on Social Attachment and Love," *Psychoneuroendocrinology* 23, no. 8 (1998): 779–818.

39. Meg Meekere, M.D., *Epidemic: How Teen Sex Is Killing Our Kids* (New York: LifeLine Press, 2002), 182–186.

40. Chap Clark, *Hurt: Inside the World of Today's Teenagers* (New York: Baker, 2004), 39–56.

41. Commission on Children at Risk. "Hardwired to Connect: The New Scientific Case for Authoritative Communities," *Institute for American Values* (2003): 23.

42. Barbara Strauch, *The Primal Teen* (New York: Anchor Books, 2003), 96.

43. Resnick, Bearman, Blum, et al., "Protecting Adolescents from Harm."

44. Strauch, *The Primal Teen*, 149.

Chapter 7: Final Thoughts

1. J. N. Giedd, J. Blumenthal, N. O. Jeffries, F.X. Castellanos, H. Liu, A. Zijdenbos, T. Paus, A. C. Evans and J. L Rapoport, "Brain development during childhood and adolescence: a longitudinal MRI study," *Nature Neuroscience* (1999): 2(10): 861–63.

2. M. Beauregard, "Mind does really matter: evidence from neuroimaging studies of emotional self-regulation, psychotherapy, and placebo effect," *Progress in Neurobiology* (Mar. 2007): 81(4):218-36.

Charles A. Nelson, "Neural Plasticity and Human Development: The Role of Early Experience in Sculpting Memory Systems," *Developmental Science* 3 no. 2 (2000): 115–36.

3. Larry Bumpass and Hsien–Hen Lu, "Trends in Cohabitation and Implications for Children's Family Contexts in the United States," *Popula-*

tion Studies, Vol. 54, No. 1 (Mar., 2000), 29–41.

4. Edward Laumann, Robert T. Michael, and Gina Kolata, *Sex in America* (New York: Time Warner, 1995), 127.

5. J. Debiec, "Peptides of love and fear: Vasopressin and oxytocin modulate the integration of information in the amygdale" (2005), *Bioessays* 27 (9): 869–73.

   A. Bartels, and S. Zeki (2004), "The neural correlates of maternal and romantic love," *Neuroimage* 21 (3): 1155–66.

6. L. J. Waite and M. Gallagher, *The Case for Marriage: Why Married People Are Happier, Healthier, and Better Off Financially* (New York: Doubleday, 2000), 47–123.

7. David P. Schmitt and 118 members of the International Sexuality Description Project, "Universal Sex Difference in the Desire for Sexual Variety: Tests from 52 Nations, 6 Continents, and 13 Islands."

8. N. I. Eisenberger and M. D. Lieberman, "Why Rejection Hurts: A Common Neural Alarm System for Physical and Social Pain," *Trends in Cognitive Science* 8, no. 7 (2004): 294–300.

9. *Guidelines for Comprehensive Sexuality Education*, 3rd ed. (National Guidelines Task Force, The Sexuality Information and Education Council for the United States, 2004).

INDEX

Abstinence
  happiness and, 119, 129
  teenagers' views of, 89–90, 106, 137
Abuse, sexual, 84
Activities for young people, 126–27
Adult guidance. *See* Guidance
Alcohol and drugs, 123
Appetite, 14–15
Assertiveness, 122
Awakening, 13–14
Axons, 27

BDNF (brain-derived neurotrophic factor), 85
Behavior change, 19, 106–8, 116, 119–20
Birth control, 12, 84
Bonding
  in broken relationships, 54–56, 85, 87
  in cohabiting couples, 96–99
  during intercourse, 77
  need for inborn, 82
  oxytocin and, 36–38, 40–41, 45, 105
  vasopressin and, 41–43, 106

Boundaries, 124
Boys, sexual abuse of, 86–87
Brain
    BDNF (brain-derived neurotrophic factor), 85
    chemicals, tracking, 26
    decision-making and, 21
    judgment and, 51, 113
    as moldable/adaptable, 29–30, 35, 53–54, 93, 107
    neurogenesis, 107
    neurons, 27–29
    neuroscientific research on, 21, 50, 51
    overview, 45–46
    prefontal cortex, 33, 51, 102, 103, 124
    remolding, 107–8
    as sex organ, 25–26, 45
    sexual excitement and, 16
    support cells, 27
    synapses, 27–28, 29, 30, 31
Breakups
    reasons for, 55, 64
    results of, 77–79, 104–6
Brizendine, Louann, 39
Broken relationships, 54, 55, 85

Centers for Disease Control and Prevention, 85
Children
    childhood sexual abuse, 86, 87
    connectedness in, 60
    mirror neurons and, 60
    in stable marriages, 42
Coan, James, 67
Cohabitation, 96–99
Commitment
    in cohabiting relationships, 97

premarital sex and, 80
Condoms, 12, 81, 84, 88
Connectedness, 59–63
Contraceptives, 12, 81, 121
Cytoplasm, 27

Date rape, 86, 89
Decision making, 21, 69, 107, 113, 114
Dendrites, 27
Denmark, South Carolina, 118–19
Depression/suicide attempts, 20, 78, 79
Disease, 12, 15, 79, 81, 117
Divorce, 80, 101
Doidge, Norman, 107
Doing what is natural, 108
Dopamine
    addictive drugs similarity, 35, 76
    functions of, 31–34, 75, 106
    providing excitement/action, 32–34, 66
    "reward signal" action, 32, 34, 77
    risk and, 34, 35
    role of in adolescents, 33, 34

Endorphins, 31
Eriksson, Peter, 107
Estrogen, 14, 31
Evolution, 136–37

Galynaker, Igor, 86
Goleman, Daniel, 60
Gonorrhea, 117
Guidance, community-centered, 118–19
Guidance, parent/mentor
    impact of, 19, 112–18

importance of, 57, 58
reasons for, 90–91
See also Parents

Happiness, 95, 99, 114, 119, 129
Health
     in close sexual relationships, 66–67
     in high-conflict relationships, 67
Herpes, 81, 82
HIV/AIDS, 15
Home environment, 19
Hooking up, 100, 101
Hormones, 14, 19, 75

Infatuation, 62, 63, 64
Infection
     disclosure of, 80
     potential, 17
     See also STDs (sexually transmitted diseases)
Intercourse, 54, 76, 101

Judgment, maturity for, 51, 112

Kiecolt-Glaser, Janice K., 66

Lakewood, California, 88
Living together. *See* Cohabitation
Love, 63, 66, 67, 69
Lust, 67–69

Magnetic Resonance Imaging (MRI), 50, 51, 133–34, 136
Manipulation, sexual, 87–88
Marriage
     care of children and, 42

oxytocin and, 37–38
premarital sex and, 101–2
providing stability/success, 94, 95
relationship health and, 56, 63
Mature judgment, 51, 52
McNeely, C., 112
Mentoring. *See* Guidance, parent/mentor; Parents
"Mirror neurons," 59–60
Molestation, 86, 87
Monogamous, non-marital relationships
characteristics of, 63, 99–100
risks of, 99
MRI (Magnetic Resonance Imaging), 50, 51, 133–34, 136
Multiple sexual partners
age first sex experience and, 76
high school/college students, 100–101

National Campaign to Prevent Teen Pregnancy (NCTP), 89, 106
Neurochemicals, 30–43
Neurogenesis, 107
Neurons
connections of, 27–28
described, 27
"mirror neurons," 59–60
neurogenesis, 107
Neuroscience research techniques
breakthroughs in, 26
MRI (Magnetic Resource Imaging), 50, 51, 133–34, 136
recommendations from, 136, 138–39
Nurturing, 59, 60

Oral sex, 75, 81, 101
Oxytocin

action of, 36
bonding caused by, 36–38, 41, 45
dilemmas caused by, 40–41
reasons for release of, 36
trust built by, 39

Parents
 guidance/counsel by, 112–18, 120–21
 impact of on behavior, 112, 116
 letting go, 127–28
 as role models, 117
 "The Talk," 116
Peck, Scott M., 108
Pedophiles, 86, 87
PET scan, 50–51
Pheromones, impact of, 44
Physical contact, limiting, 123
Prefrontal cortex, 33, 51, 102, 103, 124
Pregnancy
 cohabiting couples and, 97
 contraceptives/condoms and, 83
 out-of-wedlock, 12, 81, 82
Premarital sex, 80, 94, 101–2
Progesterone, 31
Promiscuity, 137
Puberty, 14, 19

Quinsey, Vernon, 87

Rape, 84, 86, 88, 89
Rationalizations, 93–94
Regrets, 105–106
Relationships
 broken, 85, 86

connectedness of, 58–61
intact/stable, 56
marriages as, 66–67
mature/immature, 65, 66
parent/mentor guidance and, 53–58
stages of, 62–63
Remolding, 107, 108
Resnick, Michael D., 121
"Reward signal" action, dopamine, 32, 34, 76
Risks
dopamine and, 34, 35
of hooking up, 100, 101
necessity of, 54
of premarital sex, 94, 101–2
of short-term sexual relationships, 54–56, 63
of substance abuse, 89
Rizzolatti, Giacomo, 59
The Road Less Traveled (Peck), 108
Rules, abiding by, 88

Schore, Allan N., 59
Serotonin, 31
Seventeen, 61
Sex
benefits, 94, 95
as connectedness, 58–62, 103, 104, 105
defined, 15–17
human *vs.* animal, 102–5
love and, 63, 66, 67, 69
as lust, 67–68

Sexual abuse, 84–89
Sexual activity
abstaining from, suggestions, 121–23

as addictive, 35, 77, 101, 105
adolescent, ramifications of, 20
brain and, 16
definition, 16
high school/college, 100–101
infection potential, 17
normalization of nonmarital, 74
overview, 16–18
parental disapproval of, 121
sequence of events, 16–17
"Sexual awakening," 13, 14
Sexual coercion, 84–89
Sexual entanglement, avoiding, 121–23
Sexual intercourse
    bonding during, 54, 76
    normal behavior, 74–75
    oxytocin and, 36–37
Sexual manipulation, 87–89
Sexually transmitted diseases (STDs), 12, 15, 79, 81, 117
Short-term sexual relationships, 54–56, 63, 105–6
Significant others, 95, 96
Spur Posse, 86
Statistics
    on contraceptives, 83
    depression/suicide attempts, 78, 79
    multiple sexual partners, 74
    sex outside of marriage, 75–76
    STD cases, American, 81
    on unmarried teen mothers, 82
STDs (sexually transmitted diseases), 12, 15, 79, 81, 117
Suicide attempts, 20, 78, 79
Support cells, 27
Synapses, 27–28, 30, 53
Syphilis, 117

Testosterone, 14, 19, 31
Trust, 39–40

Vaccines, 12
Values, 122
Vasopressin, 41, 42, 43, 45
Viral sexually transmitted diseases, 117
Virginity, 119

TheMedicalInstitute

This book is the product of research conducted at The Medical Institute for Sexual Health.

To learn more about issues involving sexual health, log on to www.medinstitute.org or dial 800-892-9484.

The Medical Institute for Sexual Health (MI) is a non-profit (501c3) medical, educational, and research organization. MI was founded to confront the global epidemics of teen pregnancy and sexually transmitted infections (STIs). MI identifies and evaluates scientific information on sexual health and promotes healthy sexual decisions and behaviors by communicating credible scientific information.